Pieces of Dreams

Pieces of Dreams

Eleven Minutes

Michael H Fiondella Jr

Cover Illustration
Rai Fiondella

Proud Daughter Publishing
Alger, MI

Copyright © 2025 Mike Fiondella

All rights reserved. No part of this publication may be reproduced, distributed or transmitted in any form or by any means, including photocopying, recording, or other electronic or mechanical methods, without the prior written permission of the publisher, except in the case of brief quotations embodied in critical reviews and certain other noncommercial uses permitted by copyright law. For permission requests, please write to the publisher.

Marion J Chard/Proud Daughter Publishing
1460 Joy St Alger, MI 48610

Publisher's Note: This written work contains memoirs of Michael Fiondella Jr. This includes but is not limited to statements and/or sayings and/or comments mentioned by relatives or others as accurately as possible. Unauthorized disclosure copying, distribution, and/or use of this written work or its contents is strictly prohibited without permission from Michael Fiondella Jr and/or immediate family members.

Book & cover design © 2025 Marion J Chard
Cover Illustration © 2025 Rai Fiondella

ISBN: 979-8-9927978-1-7
Library of Congress Control # 2025905893

Acknowledgments

Rai Fiondella - No words can express the thanks for your book cover. My wonderful daughter.

Marion Chard - I'd like to thank you for all your patience and tremendous help to edit and create this book. This would have been impossible without your efforts. (Jay, thanks for the great recommendation.)

Branwen Oshea - I'd like to thank Branwen for all the advice and help starting my book adventure and first reviews.

Drum corps members, past, present and future. Thank you.

Drum corps fans and spectators. Thanks to that wonderful salute from the Madison Scouts and the Allentown crowd to the Cadets (DCI 2024) Thank you all!

Dedicated to all the good people everywhere.

Table of Contents

Brief History	1
Early Years	9
Mr. Sturtze & Pop	35
Choosing Music	41
Next Decision	51
Emerald Cadets	59
Sixteen and Onward	67
Competition Time	99
A Successful Failure	111
1974	125
Is It Done?	135
Garfield Cadets	147
The Tour	161
The DCI Finals	171
Moving On	179
Epilogue	185

Preface

Based on a true story of Hope, Faith, Family, and Young Memories, I will, to the best of my ability and, as memory permits, chronologically pace through some memoirs from the beginning of my life with experiences that will eventually lead to a unique and incredible musical adventure. This particular experience would test the boundaries that include but are not limited to physical stamina, musicianship, dedication, discipline, and passion. What I believe to be a very different kind of experience, I included a more all-encompassing story that incorporates many memories of my family, various childhood adventures, and numerous events that will provide a more in-depth look at the chosen path.

I was extremely fortunate to have a strong, loving, and wonderful family and group of friends. Hopefully, those less fortunate have someone or others who can be supportive. There is someone for everyone out there, although it can take considerable time to find the person or people you truly trust. One needs to have hope & faith.

This is a memoir of a young person's deep passion and the dream of possibly performing in an exclusive musical event. Although music still plays an integral part in my life, the book focuses on when I was approximately seven to twenty-one. This includes learning, performing, teaching, and loving music, more specifically, rudimental drumming in my formative years, and how I was fortunate to have a wonderful family whose influence led to the chance (even though brief) of performing on a grand musical stage. Nonetheless, I would be neglectful if I did not include at least a short family history to make the story more wholesome. After all, this is how I became who I am.

However, this story does not reflect on my later life, subsequent career, or my wonderful and most important immediate family: my wife Jennifer, my sons Michael and Nicholas, my daughter Mary Rosaline, and our angel, whom we will see someday. It also doesn't cover my delightful and faithful dogs through the years, Pepper, Sheba, Luna, Zoey, and Bella (and more will probably follow in the years to come). These are simply some young memories about a childhood dream and goal and what I believe to have been a unique experience. Sometimes, you need the attitude and motivation not to give up on the things you love. Even though I am not a professional writer, if presenting this means it might help someone in any way, then it is well worth the effort. Having a deep passion for something and making at least some effort can be a great experience. Trying has worth, no matter the consequences, as long as it is for the good of things.

The remote chance to perform in arguably the best and most spectacular musical marching competition that highly challenged the mental, physical, and musical levels (at least in the 1970s) was a very misunderstood and unfamiliar genre to the majority of the general public and inarguably an activity with substantial growing pains. And I'm hoping that the words on the following pages can express what I wish to pass along. Every generation—and every person—has their hopes and dreams. To possibly be a part of a top drum and bugle corps military style art form, along with its very intense preparations, including all-day rehearsals all summer long without any compensation – that's right, no pay — was an honor and a rite of passage for me. It was a deep-rooted passion to perform in one big show that combined superb athletic ability with musical excellence. In some ways, it can be said that it took many years, or in my case, at least fourteen years of hard work, to have an isolated chance to perform a captivating show that would only last for a short eleven minutes. Unpaid, unknown, and criticized by some, yet highly appreciated by others, it presented something at its best, found nowhere else. It might have been fate, luck, determination, answered prayers, or a combination to have a chance (at least make one attempt under some very unusual circumstances) to perform in the largest show of its kind. But as we all know, life sometimes gets in the way. Therefore, I'm so fortunate to share this with you in these pieces of dreams.

Brief History

My mother and father's families were extremely hard-working Americans of Italian descent. Many would be surprised by the early Italian American experience, especially those hailing from the southern part of the peninsula (but I'm confident all people have fascinating stories to share).

My mother cannot be described in words. She was an angel. Mom was so wonderful to everyone; words could never do her justice. She was a beautiful human being. My father was a very hard worker and an incredible provider. My brother Bill, whom I probably looked up to more than he realized, was an excellent, strong, and caring person who worked hard at everything he did. Besides his usual work, he was involved in ambulance work, working as a fireman, fire marshal, auxiliary state policeman, and EMT.

Mom's Dad, whom we called Pop (William Giordano), who many considered the cornerstone of my immediate family, was a good and strong person. Grandma Giordano was another angel. Some might consider this an overabundance of "too good to be true," but any other way to speak would not be accurate.

Michael H Fiondella Jr

Many of my father's side of the family (the Fiondellas) lived a few towns away. Numerous people on my mother's side (the Giordanos) lived in the same neighborhood where I grew up. Many in my mom's family purchased small homes around the same time in the 1950s, during the suburban housing boom after WW2, in Wallingford, Connecticut.

Pop was born in America, and for various reasons, his family moved back to Italy until he returned in his teenage years. Pop played many instruments exceptionally well and was in the Hershey Band in the early 1900s. Milton Hershey helped provide the instruments and what was needed for the band. He and his family would often watch them perform. Pop also played clarinet in the Royal Italian Band in Harrisburg, Pennsylvania. Grandma Giordano was an amazing person who always saw the good in people. Such a beautiful, peaceful person.

Pop was a stone cutter. This included building and cutting granite fireplaces and monuments. One of the individuals who started the Giordano Bros. Monuments was located right next to Yale University in New Haven, Connecticut.

Grandfather Fiondella was a cabinetmaker. Like many others, he was born in Italy and faced incredible challenges in those days. Grandma Fiondella was a determined, hard worker. She had a huge garden that was always well taken care of. I recall her noticing every weed in a small garden I cared for at my house. During one of her visits to my home, she walked out to the small garden where I worked and turned to my father, saying something in Italian. Translating, my father said, "You need to get rid of the weeds."

Pieces of Dreams

Grandpa Fiondella, whom I never met, moved to America to seek a better life. America was the land of opportunity. I know my grandparents and my parents faced enormous challenges, and because of them, my life was much better than theirs, to say the least. I'm sure all of them had stories, too.

During the Great Depression, my father knew he had to do something to improve his life and help others. One of the things he decided to do was join the United States Navy, which he did at the earliest age possible, at seventeen or eighteen. It was his honor to serve. He sent money home to his family to help during these difficult times. In May of 1937, my dad's ship was sent to the crash site of the Hindenburg disaster. The Porter-class Navy destroyer, the USS McDougal (DD-358), was also part of the search party for Amelia Earhart in 1937. On August 10, 1941, the destroyer escorted President Franklin D. Roosevelt to and from the HMS Prince of Wales to meet with Prime Minister Winston Churchill to discuss the solidarity between the U.S. and Great Britain against the Axis aggression. I remember hearing a story about one of his visits home after being away for a while in the Navy. His father saw him on Whiting Street in Hamden, Connecticut. He got so excited seeing him that he ran as fast as he could to greet him all the way down the street.

It took some time, but Dad kept asking Mom to date him until she finally accepted. Later, Mom and Dad married on September 1, 1941.

December 7, 1941, the attack on Pearl Harbor, would, of course, alter history as we knew it. My father was already in the Navy. His ship served throughout the war on several tasks. Many of my uncles also served. Uncle George Fiondella, among others, served in the Army. I'm pretty sure Uncle George received the Purple Heart, and Uncle Cappie (my father's sister's husband) was wounded in the front lines of Italy. My Uncle William Giordano (my mom's brother) was a POW for several years. He was caught in Africa and held in a German prison camp. My Uncle Ed Baker (husband to Aunt Millie, mom's sister) was in the Army and was involved in the battles of Iwo Jima and Guadalcanal. I recall Uncle Ed having a beat-up shoe box with many medals from the war (I recognized one as the bronze star).

I believe he destroyed one or two pillboxes while he was already wounded. All these relatives never discussed the war much, so I tried to recall some history as best as possible. My Uncle William, my mom's brother, eventually wrote a book, or at least had a draft of his POW experience. All these previous experiences could be novels by themselves, and here I am trying to explain what I recall about these absolutely incredible events in this short segment.

Several of my aunts worked in factories. My Aunt Carrie actually lost part of a finger while working. My Aunt Millie Baker (my mom's sister and wife of my Uncle Ed) was a nurse at Yale New Haven Hospital and was quite good at what she did. My Uncle Walter (mom's younger brother) had a beautiful operatic voice. He also served in the Army. I know something awful happened to him during WW2, as he was in a veterans' hospital for the rest of his life after the war. I remember visiting him at the hospital and when he was home at Pops for visits. Uncle Walter was such a peaceful person. I can't imagine what Pop and Grandma went through with one son in a prison camp and one ending up in a hospital.

There's one sad moment I recall when visiting him at the Veterans Hospital in Massachusetts. I was a young kid, and I waited on a small bench for my grandparents and parents as they went inside to get Uncle Walter. They must have had a small bazaar or some game time for the veterans in a small area before me. During one contest, a person would have to hammer a nail partly into a board. One middle-aged man desperately tried to get the nail to stay on that board, but could not. I remember feeling so sad. The person running the booth snuck in and helped him win. He was so happy to win that prize, jumping up and down joyfully. That moment will stick with me for my entire life.

My parents and grandparents continued to teach me never to complain, to move forward, and to help others when possible. I try to remember their advice, but I don't think I follow it as much as I should.

Some Italians were placed in internment camps, but at the same time, Italian Americans made up the most significant percentage of the American Army in WW2.

Obviously, we all have trying times in our lives. My Grandma and Dad's mom were no exception. My cousin Gloria (Uncle Joe's daughter) explained what happened to Uncle Michael, whom I never met. She said he was a delightful kid, always smiling no matter what, and a very handsome young man. Evidently, when Michael was thirteen, he caught pneumonia. In those days, there were no antibiotics for that. He ended up passing away. I can't imagine this. Years later, she would name my father Michael after him. Michael, my father, was also a pleasant soul and always had a smile, was filled with laughter, and had fun, no matter what, and was handsome too.

I'm not sure how far back the music goes in my family. I was told that my great-grandfather, Michael Fiondella, incorporated a flute into sheep-herding in Italy. To the best of my knowledge, he wished to hand this flute down to all the Michaels in the family and, if not, to someone with a love of music. It's a unique family treasure.

My Dad had a cousin who was popular publicly. I never met this gentleman but heard many wonderful stories about him. Unfortunately, I don't believe my father saw him that often, or at least not since I was born. His name was Jay Fiondella. He was born on August 6, 1926. He also acted and appeared in movies and shows, including Gunsmoke, Perry Mason, Batman, Mission Impossible, Fantasy Land, and Lethal Weapon. He was the co-owner of Chex Jay bar and restaurant on the Santa Monica Pier in southern California, which was started in 1959. He briefly shared a place with Leonard Nimoy when he first visited Los Angeles. His restaurant was known to serve many celebrities, and supposedly, he would kick out anyone who would pester them. He was involved in treasure hunting and had gained great reviews for the restaurant. Many celebrities like Henry Kissinger, Marlon Brando, and Alan Shepard would go there, who supposedly brought one of the restaurant's peanuts to the moon. Also, Steve McQueen, Frank Sinatra, Sammy Davis Jr, Dean Martin,

Pieces of Dreams

Marilyn Monroe, Judy Garland, Lee Marvin, Robert Stack, Natalie Wood, Warren Beatty, Elizabeth Taylor, Johnny Carson, Nancy Sinatra, Clint Eastwood, Michelle Pfeiffer, Mel Gibson, Jerry Seinfeld, Sean Penn, Drew Barrymore, Richard Burton, Richard Harris, Peter Sellers, Jim Morrison, Jim Brown, Jane Fonda, Don Drysdale, Hugh Hefner, Joe DiMaggio, Cary Grant, Buzz Aldrin, the Beach Boys, and many other sports figures and politicians such as Henry Kissinger.

I was fortunate enough to speak with him later in life. I was interested in how to make contact or get advice on approaching those involved in the movie and writing business. I telephoned and explained to the young lady (who answered), stating I was a distant relative, and asked if I could speak briefly with Jay. She was very gracious, as Jay was. It would be the only time I would talk with him and how welcoming he was. My dad also understood that even though he treated everyone nicely, he would give special attention to anyone who visited from his home state of Connecticut.

I was the youngest in my immediate family. It's surreal that as I write this, I once belonged to such a large family. At one point, an article was written about us showing five generations around Easter time—Shane Fiondella, 2 1/2 months, father William Fiondella Jr., grandfather William Fiondella Sr, great-grandmother Mrs. Michael Fiondella, and great-great-grandmother Mrs. William Giordano. Now, my parents, uncles, aunts, and brother are gone.

My brother Bill and I used to tease each other when we were the only two left. I have faith that I will see everyone again someday. You need to have hope and faith. Seeing how terrible people can be, you'd think that they do not care about anyone. But I believe the good outweighs the bad. I think it's common sense to see that there is good and evil in different people, places, countries, and generations. Heroes also exist in every generation. I feel, as a whole, it will be difficult, if not impossible, to match the WW2 generation. I am one of the last individuals directly connected to the WW2 generation since my father. So many of my uncles were directly involved in that war. This memoir is meant to be uplifting, but life takes many turns that sometimes get in the way.

Well, there you have it. Ever so brief notes regarding my family history.

Early Years

It was Christmas morning in the late 1950s, one of my first memories when I was about four years old (and as I'd later learn, Dad would dress up like Santa and was a jolly old man). I woke up early with great excitement. I turned to my big brother Bill and said, "I'll race you to the Christmas tree." I think he let me win.

I remember seeing Pop, directing music to a record at one of our many great, fun family get-togethers. He looked like a conductor leading an orchestra. He loved music, and one of his favorite songs was 76 Trombones.

Often, when Mom and Dad ventured out, Pop and Grandma (who lived next door) would babysit. I remember watching Jackie Gleason on that small black-and-white television or playing checkers with Pop. Sometimes, he would "fix" it (so he would win) just to get a reaction out of me.

Mom and Pop began to teach me the basics of music, but little did I realize where this would lead me. They both taught me some music notation, and Pop taught me how to play the mandolin and some basic drumming skills, while Mom gave me piano lessons.

We lived on a steep hill, and the kids would take to the snow in the winter with our sleds. I remember Mom bundling me up so well that I could barely move. Once, a bunch of us were sliding down in a line when I spotted a car parked down below, and I yelled to my buddies, "Hey guys, move over." And someone replied, "I can't; we're going too fast." Therefore, there was no way to avoid it, and yes, you might have guessed it, I ran right under that old car. Good thing Mom had me bundled up, but I ended up stuck and couldn't move. However, a big kid (well, at least to us) came out of a house and pulled me out by my legs, which were partially sticking out. One of my friends said, "Look, he's not even crying." Ah, thanks to many layers of clothes...

When Chubby Checker's The Twist was popular, Dad and Mom would ask me to dance at family gatherings. They got a kick out of a five-year-old twisting the night away. I was told that brother Bill got to be on Dick Clark's American Bandstand. Bill was actually an excellent dancer, and when he was young, the word was that he could tap. I only saw him tap a few beats once when I was about ten, and it was pretty awesome; however, he never went far with it. I recall my cousin Joan, Dad, and Bill always smiling, laughing, and dancing at all the parties. They were actually great dancers, too.

I was at a party at Uncle William's one summer. He had worked diligently to make his beat-up yard a wonderful, beautiful area, and it showed. A bridge with roses grew over the sides and spanned a small stream. After crossing the bridge, a small outside stairway led up to a flat area with a granite barbecue grill and a great party setup. At one party, my cousin Mary Ann and I were sitting at the small kid's bench, and Pop somehow squeezed in on the opposite side so he could be there with us. Pop made us laugh as usual, and we had fun as always. This same bench was entirely loaded with great food and drinks, and I'm smiling and just thinking about that moment. Such fun. Then Pop decided to get up, and as he arose, Mary Ann and I started falling backward while all the food, drinks, plates, and whatever else was on that table flew at us. While Mary Ann and I laughed so hard, Pop, Mom, and a host of adults ran over to help. Pop felt so bad, but we just laughed and laughed and laughed. Why do I remember times much more clearly than others? I do not know. However, this one I remember lucidly. I guess it would not be easy to forget.

When I was about five or six, Pop rode me in his car down a bumpy road that led to Mike's Barbershop near Sleeping Giant Park. Mike was a relative (maybe Pop's cousin?). I loved that ride, hitting the bumps and bouncing in the seat. I was always so happy and full of laughter while with him. "I want a Beatles haircut," I declared, sitting in the chair. However, Mike, the barber, and Pop said something to each other in Italian, after which Mike, the barber, buzzed my head. "What happened to my Beatles haircut?" I yelled. "Now-you-gotta-John-a-Glen-a-haircut-like-a-the-astronaut," Pop replied. What? Oh, well, I was always intrigued by astronauts.

Michael H Fiondella Jr

I was lucky to have the mom and dad I had. In or about 1960, there was quite a storm. Maybe it was a hurricane because I recall the dark skies and wicked wind, and being upset because my little chair was outside on our small patio. Guess what? They went out in that terrible weather to get my chair so I would calm down. I also remember losing a tooth and being upset, and Mom getting me ready for kindergarten and drying my tears. She was always there for me.

I enjoyed some sports as a kid. Playing baseball, I recall being up to bat and someone yelling, "You stink." That got me so frustrated. I was no Mickey Mantle or Roger Maris, but as the next pitch was heading in my direction, I decided to close my eyes and swing as hard as I could. Bang! The ball made it right into the glove of the center fielder, but he dropped it, so I made it to base. Lots of cheers. However, I do not recommend closing your eyes.

For some strange reason, I clearly remember being at a fair. I must have been about five or six years old and sitting on a merry-go-round, mesmerized, watching the bass drum and clanging of the band organ in 3/4-time. Before you think this is crazy, I'm just telling you what I remember. It completely captivated me. Boom, clang, clang, boom, clang, clang, with a monkey jangling the cymbals. Again, it was one of those random recollections with my mother. But it seems that any music swept me in.

Unfortunately, around the same period, I remember seeing the basement of Parker Farms Elementary School, probably for the only time in my life. We were practicing for an air raid emergency during the Cuban Missile

Crisis(?), so it was perhaps first grade. I was happy that the adults decided not to start any trouble. I would learn later that it was a pretty serious time. Wow.

On one field trip, we visited a bread-making facility—I think it was Wonder Bread. We had spaghetti for lunch. The teachers got a kick out of me twirling my spaghetti neatly with my fork. When they remarked on this, I explained that my grandfather Pop taught me how to eat spaghetti properly.

Ah, yes, now for the infamous first bee sting. I was outside playing, minding my own business, when I noticed a bee crawling on my foot. I just stared at it, wondering. Then without any provocation, the dang thing bent its butt and laid the stinger in me. Of course, I ran into the house, yelling ouch and screaming, while Mom calmed me down as usual, while my Aunt Millie, the nurse, checked my throat and face. I didn't know it then, but she was looking for possible swelling (an allergic reaction). "Why are you looking at my throat? I got stung on my foot?" I stammered. "Don't worry," she replied, smiling.

Visits were fun to Hamden and North Haven, Connecticut, especially during the holidays, to see Grandma Fiondella, Uncle Cappie, Aunt Carrie, Uncle Sal, Auntie Ann, Uncle Joe, Aunt Loretta, Uncle George, Auntie Irene, and their daughters Bobian and Georgian. Georgian had such a funny, unforgettable laugh. We would see the Giordano side of the family more often as we lived in the immediate area with Pop, Grandma, Uncle William, Aunt Hilda, Uncle Eddie, and Aunt Millie. We frequently visited Uncle Walter at Grandma's house next door or the Veterans Hospital in Massachusetts.

I was told stories about Aunt Mary, Uncle Joe's first wife, who passed away when I was a baby. Unfortunately, I do not remember much because I was only two. Still, every time I saw her, they said I would light up like a bulb. There must have been something about her. My Uncle Joe's wife, Loretta, was close to my mom; she was such a pleasant person, and my mom would spend lots of time with her. I recall one event when they returned from a shopping trip. Mom was a perfect driver and angel. Someone must have cut her off while driving, but as usual, Mom stayed silent. However, Aunt Loretta yelled, "Where did you get your license? At Sears and Roebuck?"

Another fond memory was visiting Grandma Fiondella as a small child and hearing the record by Alvin and the Chipmunks, Christmas Don't Be Late.

Another Christmas Eve memory is around 1966, when a big snowstorm hit Connecticut. I remember many from the neighborhood out sledding at night down on our big hill on the street, and many walking around the neighborhood talking and wishing everyone a Merry Christmas.

Dad and I visited Uncle William and Uncle Eddie's home. Those are still warm and wonderful memories. No computers and phones to distract us. Just good ol' conversation and being in the moment. Maybe I'm older and dull now, or too many phones and computers are vying for our attention. I did work with computers in some fashion as an electrical engineer, but I'm never glued to them. Seeing so many people talking and smiling, having fun, and interacting with each other was so special.

Elvis Presley was a huge hit, of course, and what talent. That itself could fill a few paragraphs. Speaking of impressionable moments, I remember The Beatles' first appearance on the Ed Sullivan Show. I also remember being so annoyed while trying to watch their movie, Help, in the small theatre on Center Street in Wallingford, Connecticut, as all the girls continually screamed. Another memorable experience? Recalling Mom and Dad yelling for me to watch this guy called Buddy Rich. It may have been the Merv Griffin show, and I was in awe. Oh, what a drummer. Boy, he could play!

Mom was a tremendous pianist. After many years of not playing very often (probably due to being a mom), I remember her picking up the music and suddenly playing The Burning of Rome (March) by E.T. Paull (1903). She played everything: classical, rock, pop, and more. I'm not biased when I say she was incredible. Learning a little piano from her, however, I never appreciated that experience until now.

Every Sunday morning, there were donuts at Pops. All in the Family would be there, and the house was filled with joy, laughter, and teasing. Games and music, and it was loud! Music was always playing regardless of the time or event. We usually had to convince Mom to play at our house or Uncle William and Aunt Hilda's, where a piano was present. My Uncle William also played piano pretty well. Crazy but fun times, and I'm glad I had the chance to experience the little but finer things in life.

Michael H Fiondella Jr

Since my brother was already married when I was about five or six, I was, in essence, an only child. I was lucky to have a great brother and a terrific family, but the two I hung around with were my neighborhood friends, Rick and John.

For some reason, the drums captivated me. I started bugging Mom and Dad about taking drum lessons, and I wonder now what they thought of my yearnings.

Finally, at about seven years of age, I received my first drumsticks and pad with great excitement. I still treasure the pad, but I do not recall what happened to the pair of sticks from Pop. I wound up taking a few drum set lessons from instructor Ray across town, a kind and patient teacher. I did play and practice, but never enough or in a formal way.

Spending lots of time playing records and banging on bar stools and boxes was still fun. It was my first "set of drums." Dad seemed okay with that. In fifth grade at Parker Farms Elementary School, I recall the teachers asking if anyone would like to learn an instrument. I immediately raised my hand and asked, "Can I take drum lessons?" With an annoyed look, the answer was, "No drums will be taught as lessons here." Sigh! My energy level was above average, and I always wanted to know why! This might be a bad habit I still have...

One day, one of the teachers said, "If you need to know the spelling of a word, use the dictionary." I raised my hand and asked, "How are we supposed to look up the word if we can't spell it?" I earned another unique look as she replied, "Guess a little." On one of my report cards, the teacher noted, "At times, Michael is in a world of his own." I think this may have been because I would often daydream about performing in a big show where everyone would be cheering. Oh well. I did show respect, though, as I was taught.

Dad worked in plumbing and heating, and when he came home from work, he was often exhausted, yet never complained. Mom had everything perfect in the home.

My father had a cousin from Italy who was a priest, and Dad would speak Italian to him, translating for me. During one visit to America, I asked him if he liked girls. Amusement was followed by laughter, and then a lengthy discussion in Italian ensued.

At Parker Farms Elementary during second grade, Mrs. B mentioned a bus would take us caroling around Wallingford. Usually, anything with music interested me, and many of my friends and I decided to go. For some reason, I remembered this time because it seemed so peaceful, and I recall thinking that someday, far in the future, I might look back on this. One thing that made me have these thoughts was when I was looking out the bus window after making a stop on our tour. Many kids were talking about Mrs B because we wondered why she was crying during our excursion. I realized later in life how innocent and naïve children are. Now, I assume she was crying happy tears.

Well, this brings to mind an event that's not so innocent. I really don't remember what I did wrong. Even some of the names escape me. Anyway, the two 6th-grade teachers said they demanded to see me in their rooms after school.

To us, they were tough guys and good teachers, but strict. Of course, they must have plotted—those sneaky dudes. So, I had a decision to make. The two rooms were at the end of the hallway near one of the exits. I don't even remember the teachers' names, but I do remember the rooms. As I entered the building, I decided to go to the room on the right, and as I entered and sat down, the teacher said, "I see you chose my room." The other teacher entered that moment and asked, "Why did you choose his room over mine?" My simple answer was, "I'm more afraid of him."

I liked superhero movies. A lot of us did. One Halloween, I dressed up like Superman. I was excited to get a bunch of free candy. Who wouldn't? Mom, being Mom, would make sure someone was with us. At that time, I believe there may have been some kids who would have donned the costume and actually tried to fly. No, I honestly did not think of trying that. Mom told me, "Now remember, honey, you really cannot fly; this is make-believe." Beginning with an accent, I answered with a musical decrescendo, "MMaaaaaaaaaa!"

Uncle George (one of my father's brothers) must have known someone at the whiffle ball factory, which still exists in Connecticut. The factory would discard imperfect bats and balls due to little indentations, so sometimes, he would come over with boxes and boxes of bats and balls. One Halloween, we had so many that Pop, Grandma, and I gave them out on Halloween. The line at both houses went as far as the eye could see until we ran out.

Rick, John, and I hung around quite a bit together, and we were more like family. Eventually, we would be involved in many musically related events. John was up at bat at one whiffle ball game at Rick's house. Our yards were relatively small on those one-quarter-acre lots. No complaints here; it's just tough to play any sport in such a yard, and that's why we would usually play on a flat part of a street or in a field. Anyhow, I remember the two cars sitting in Rick's driveway. So, John cranked up and swung so hard that the small wooden bat flew out of his hands at a tremendous speed, heading straight for the driveway—the cars. The bat hit the basketball post hard and broke into two pieces, with one piece flying in between the vehicles and the other going over one car. Amazingly, nothing was hit, but I wish I had a video.

On Halloween, several friends and I decided to try something different. We sometimes pulled pranks by ringing doorbells and running away—just an innocent kids' adventure. One year, we decided to prank the kids who were pranking us, so we attempted to police the area, but we ran from them and the neighbors, who called the police. It was kind of like a kids' neighborhood watch. That was different.

A younger boy had to wear an eye patch for a long period. He seemed friendly, so I befriended him, and we'd talk about things now and then. I never thought much about it until years later, when a kid, maybe twelve, approached me as I walked home from junior high school past Parker Farms Elementary School. "Hey, remember me?" "I'm not sure, but you look familiar," I admitted. "I was the little kid with the eye patch, and you befriended me when I needed to talk to someone. So, thanks." I said, "You're welcome. I just talked, though, and it was no problem." I suppose sometimes just a little hello means something. As my grandma would say, "Treat others how you want to be treated."

Poor Dad. He had one finger on his right hand that was permanently bent at a forty-five-degree angle due to an injury in the Navy. I believe it was the left hand that was caught in a ship door(?). Anyway, I was fascinated and often tried to bend it back straight. I don't think I could count how many times I caused him pain in more than one way.

I was always interested in how things worked and needed to be active. Sometimes, I wonder how my parents dealt with my energy level. Wanting to be like Ringo, the drummer in The Beatles, I wore those black-pointed shoes that I convinced my parents to buy for me. Of course, I have always wanted to meet him, but that didn't happen.

We were neither rich nor poor, and Dad and Mom did everything they could to make ends meet. Our home was modest on that quarter acre of land, and we were a happy family. You only appreciate the things you have when they're all gone.

I recall being involved in the safety patrol and a play at Parker Farms Elementary School. The play was Death in the Antique Shop; I tried, like most, to get an easy part to have fun. No one wanted to be the main character because there were many lines to memorize. But guess what? Yup, I ended up with the central character. I worked hard to learn those lines of Mr. Pennythort! I recall the ending, pulling a fake mouse out of a chest and saying, "You women!" Everyone laughed loudly and clapped. That was a rewarding feeling that stuck with me; making people happy and cheerful, and clapping was cool. It was an interesting moment and made me think more about someday being involved in some significant performance.

Playing football—what fun! My brother and neighbor were the coaches. Years later, my brother and father would tell me about my first great tackle and how I got super excited after it happened. Participating in teamwork was a lot of fun, and it affected me even more when music was involved.

Other young memories include visiting the 1964 World's Fair in New York and seeing the giant globe. The theme was "Peace through Understanding." Something that's always needed, right?

Dad and Mom always taught me to respect people no matter who they are or where they come from, especially those who are good to others, and this will never change because it is fundamental. I believe that anyone who knew my family would agree. I lost count of how many times my mom would ask my friends how they were, and when they visited, she would almost always ask, "Would you like something to eat? Maybe a snack." She was always giving and caring, whether a meal, a sandwich, or popcorn. Many friends would tell me, "My mother wouldn't do that," or "Your mom is so nice."

One day, I recorded Pop and Grandma on my small reel-to-reel recorder, and they would play along. Pop would refer to my older brother as Billy, and we were incredibly close.

Michael & | Fiondella Jr.

The conversation I still have on tape went something like this.

Pop: "You gotta turn it up."

Grandma: "Yesterday was my birthday."

Me: "I know, Poppy, say something."

Pop with his Italian accent: "I love you, my little boy (while Grandma laughed). The best little boy I ever got. Billy, though, he's my best big boy now, Okay?"

Grandma: "Okay, Michael, I love you very much, Michael."

Me: "Okay, goodbye."

Pop: "Goodbye."

Grandma: "Goodbye."

Me: "Hi again."

Grandma: "Hi Mr Borak, how are you? Hi Mrs Borak, how are you?" (the Boraks were friends/ neighbors)

Pop: "Oh, I'm alright, I'm alright!" (answering loudly, having fun)

The way he said it made me laugh so hard, and then they laughed hard along with me.

Grandma: "I didn't say you; I said..."

Me: "Goodbye."

Grandma: "Hi, Mr and Mrs Borak. How are you?"

Pop: "You gotta talk a little louder."

Grandma: "Good, I hope."

Pop: "That, that wastes; you gotta talk."

Grandma: "You talk, you talk."

Pop: "Ooookaaaay, hooow's the boy, you know, where's Billy this time? He cut my grass yesterday, and boooy that grass was wet, and he did cut it too. Okay, gooooodbye."

Grandma: "He cut your grass..."

Pop: "Oh, he cut my grass first, then he cut your daddy's grass. Okay."

Me: "Goodbye."

Pop: "Goodbye."

It was always wonderful to see Pop and Grandma. I have so many wonderful memories. Pop gave excellent advice to my father, brother, me, and everyone. So many of us looked up to him highly. It's hard to explain in words. Remember, Mom and Pop gave me my first real exposure to music.

As time passed, I became more interested in girls. I thought Carrie (one of my neighbors a block away) was so friendly. I tried to be cool while visiting her house for a homework assignment. The main reason I remember this visit is not so much the visit itself or the homework but more because I slipped in her yard and fell right smack into her dog's poop. It was a great start to impress someone, and she tried so hard not to laugh.

There are only two girls I ever asked to marry me: my wonderful wife, Jennifer, and the other? It was a girl named Karen in the third grade. Now, I don't think she really gave me an answer, and in later years, I heard she hid in her closet when I called.

On Saturdays at Parker Farms Elementary School, they used to show movies like Laurel & Hardy's March of the Wooden Soldiers. I got such a thrill watching that. Seeing those wooden soldiers marching to get the bad guys was so exciting, with that classical music in the background.

I was involved in the Cub Scouts for a short time. I remember a den leader who was my friend Tim's mom. It must have been so different for him because she was his mother, and at that time, moms were rarely den leaders. She was a blast. We did something different once, and she took us to see the movie Those Magnificent Men in Their Flying Machines. What fun we had that day.

I enjoyed summer the most. It's not that school was terrible, but I was free to do all sorts of things more often, including playing the drums.

Rick and I were heading somewhere and jumped over a small farm fence. After taking a few steps, we noticed a big bull, and it turned to face us. Jumping the fence took little skill and motivation.

However, there were some unique winter memories, too. I recall a few instances, in particular, after an ice storm. One occurred when Rick and I decided (against our better judgment) to take our sleds to what we called the Christmas tree, deep in the woods near our homes. It was a curvy path. We thought this could be fun, but wondered about the slick pathway. However, off we went, with me being first on the trail. So, there I was, gaining speed and curving around the trees, heading downward. No helmets—nothing back then. Just before exiting the woods, the last section had four giant trees, two on each side of the path, so you would go towards the left in between two, then immediately right in between the other two. Once through, you would hit a big gully, sending you airborne, out of the woods, and down a steep hill. That was usually fun, except this time, because the ice intensified the speed. So, heading towards those last four trees, this is not looking too good. Sure enough, I didn't quite make it, and as I slid, I hit all four of them, bouncing back and forth with my flexible flyer. Bang! Bang! Bang! Bang! Then, it all ended as the front of the sled jammed into the ditch. Bang!

There, I was frozen in time and in shock. But then I heard Rick yelling, "I can't slow down; get out of the way!" Despite still being in shock, I had no choice but to roll off my sled, using it as a shield. Hey, it's nothing personal, but I didn't want to get killed. Then I heard, "Ahhhhh!!" Quickly followed by Bang! Bang! Bang! Bang! Then, there was a sliding sound and another bang into my sled. Now, we were both groaning in pain. Fortunately, nothing was broken, including our bones. We stood shaking and said, "I'm going home now."

The other ice-sliding incident had no witnesses. I'm unsure why I slid down our steep road, as it was pure ice. I'm sure Dad and especially Mom had no idea how icy it really was, and I might add, neither did I.

Michael H Fiondella Jr

I was gaining too much speed as I turned one corner from my house. So, by the time I passed that spot where I got stuck under the car years earlier, I had to do something to stop the sled, so I decided to run into my Aunt Millie and Uncle Ed's snowbank before the next turn. Hey, my aunt was a great nurse, and of course, there was no helmet again. I flew off the sled and quickly slid on my stomach across their front yard, missing the tree at the front of the house. I went home shaking and, to this day, have a scar on my left pinky finger to remind me of my insane adventure. Mom, of course, took super care of me, as usual.

Two other winter incidents... My buddy John and I tried to sled on the solid ice-surfaced snow in the cornfield near us. As we headed down that steep hill, side-by-side, my sled dug into the icy surface. I was again, as many times before, airborne or, more precisely, now, sliding down on my stomach. As we continued, I poked John, and he stared at me in amazement. I would slow down much more quickly as John continued on. Another was an infamous Toboggan run. This one is a little more complicated. A bunch of us crazies decided to overpile onto this instrument of danger and take turns in different spots on it as we took several runs down that same steep farm hill on this unique day. Well, of course, when I had my turn on the rear end of the infamous Toboggan, the dang thing decided to turn 180 degrees, so we were now heading down at a fast speed but backward. Speaking of butt, mine was sticking out slightly over the back side during this event. Of course, on this particular run down the hill, we were directly following one of the only rocks sticking slightly out of the snow. Yes, you guessed it. My poor rear

Pieces of Dreams

end took a direct hit from that sledding device. The Toboggan and my beautiful butt hit one of the few rocks hard. The Toboggan flipped entirely over, and we all fell out everywhere. I was in excruciating pain now, having, let's say, two areas in my backside, one normal and one black and blue. I could barely walk as I held my butt in pain. A few thought it was funny until I said I must go home; I could barely walk. It took quite a while to heal.

I'm sure you've heard of Tarzan. One of the original stars I remember was Johnny Weissmuller. He was also an Olympic swimmer. I remember Dad telling me how he worked on one of his pools. Cool movies. I remember John's Dad telling him what that famous Tarzan yell, "Ungawa," meant. "Do you know what ungawa means? It means let's get the heck out of here!"

Things were so different. Friends and I would walk to Parker Farms Elementary School to see baseball games and stop at a small store called J & B's. We would load up on candy, which included candy cigarettes, bubble gum cigars, Pez, sugar straws, etc. We would trade marbles. One time, a friend in elementary school had rolls of cards that included uncut original Beatles pictures. He liked several of my marbles and, in turn, traded me three or four rolls. I can't believe I do not have them anymore, except for a few cards cut from them. I do not remember what happened to them. There were original baseball card rolls, too. All gone now.

They finally offered drum lessons at summer school at Parker Farms, and I remember the teacher there showing us "buzz" or "pressed" rolls on the snare drum. I tried to pick up drumming tips where and when I could. Hopefully, more formal lessons would come my way again later. I just kept hitting those boxes and chairs, mainly while listening to that small record player.

More memories from that period certainly included my buddy John and me creating an Apollo space project for the science fair, detailing the entire mission from launch to the moon and its return to Earth. Then, one night, a few years later, Dad and I watched the famous event (well, he slept), but as Neil Armstrong descended from the Lunar Excursion Module, I had to wake him. He opened his eyes and witnessed man's first footsteps on the moon. "That's one small step for a man, one giant leap for mankind." Then, Dad went back to sleep. We were both excited, but Dad was as tired as I was. "I remember the horse and buggy, and now we are on the moon," he'd say. What a moment.

John was a good skater. Skiing and skating were things I never got into. John asked me if I wanted to try skating and maybe some hockey on one cold winter stretch. It sounded like something different, so why not? He let me borrow a pair of skates, and we headed up to a small pond deep in the woods near our houses. There were a few logs frozen halfway out of the ice as well. So, John, a few friends, and I started. Yes, you are picturing this correctly. What in the world was I doing, attempting to play hockey for the first time on skates? I do not have an answer. I'm sure my parents would cringe to learn I was trying to play hockey.

No drama here! I remember putting on the skates, standing up, and falling. Standing up again, then falling

again. Standing up again, then falling repeatedly. You get the picture. As John tried to help me, I was finally able to skate a few feet. Then, one of the kids handed me a hockey stick. Then I tried to move the puck as someone would check me, probably just lightly, and I would fall again. After repeating this many times, I finally said, I'm done. The few kids were probably being easy on me, as best as I could remember. Still, they also enjoyed my falling again and again. No helmets, just insanity.

One car ride that came to mind with Dad was when we were driving through the center of Wallingford. The police stopped all traffic, and we were stopped right near the center of town, next to Route 5. As far as the eye could see, there were motorcycles. So, to assist with traffic, the police allowed all the bikes to pass together. I always wondered if that was during the Woodstock Music Festival in 1969 and if they were headed there.

One of our neighbors was really into motorcycles. He had this massive bike with really high handlebars. I recall him telling me that my grandfather (Pop) was always nice to him, while some others were not. He always seemed friendly to me. That's Pop for you. Unless you tried something crazy, he would always offer help, give good advice, or show kindness. Actually, that's the way my family was to everyone, always. Just don't try something terrible.

It was 1968(?). My brother Bill and Dad always worked relentlessly for years on construction. Plumbing and heating were their specialty. Dad had lots of experience and knew well what he was doing. Bill learned from him. In later years, I would learn a little, but I lacked the skills they possessed. Since Dad knew many people in the construction field and had good friends, he knew the right people to help my brother build his brand-new house on Blue Jay Drive in 1968. I remember Pop and his brother, Walter, building a gorgeous fireplace on the first floor of the split-level. I'm pretty sure it was pearl-white granite. I still remember hearing those granite chisels striking the stones over and over. I wish I had pictures of this fireplace. I wish I could go back for a few minutes to see this again and other times.

On many Saturday mornings, watching cartoons was fun, especially with Bugs Bunny, Road Runner, Tom and Jerry, Stingray, the Thunderbirds, and more. Also, many movie classics such as Abbott and Costello, Laurel and Hardy, Jerry Lewis, and so many more. Superman, Batman, and the like. I loved the Andrews Sisters. Sometimes, Rick and John would plan a time when we could watch some of these together. Mom would at least make popcorn or another snack. Warning, here comes a baby boomer thing. We did not have cell phones or cable TV, so we had to make plans by referring to the TV guide listings in the newspaper.

A few years passed as I entered Junior High School (7th-9th). Coming of age was an experience like no other, and fortunately for me, it was filled with good memories. School classes were structured differently, and school dances became appealing.

This memory is indeed stuck in my head. I was walking down a hallway, and no one was around except a special needs kid and two bullies. As I passed those three, I saw and heard those two tough bullies picking on the special-needs kid as they placed him against the lockers.

I had no clue why this was happening. I attempted to move on, minding my business without getting involved. Then I started to shake a little and thought I could not live with myself if I ignored this poor kid. I'm gonna get killed, I thought. Two against one, and they were not small. I was maybe a little bigger than average, but no Dick Butkus. As I shook and got highly frustrated, I turned and yelled loudly, "Why don't you leave him alone!" The two kids just laughed and walked away. Sweat wipe time. The special needs kid turned and politely said, "Thank you." It was a good feeling to do the right thing and help, and also, I might add, not to get the crap beaten out of me. Later, I would learn some self-defense, partly because of that experience.

Football tryouts! It was the 9th grade at Moran Junior High School. A school doctor thought he heard a heart murmur, so I had to go to Yale Hospital for a detailed exam. It was a terrifying time for me, especially in those days. This could change everything. My Aunt Millie (the great nurse) accompanied my father and me to the hospital. After undergoing several lengthy tests and seeing multiple doctors, one came into the room to talk. This doctor looked at me and said, "Have you ever heard of Dick Butkus?" I answered, "Yes, of course." She said, "Well, you have a heart like his. An athletic heart, so it is actually stronger than normal." I was confused. She continued, "It pumps so strongly at times; it may sound like something's wrong, but you actually have a strong heart. Stronger than average." I was so relieved and said, "Now, could you make me as big as Dick Butkus?"

My family continued to have some great get-togethers. So many good memories. Those times went by quickly.

For the football team, one of the rules was that we had to get a butch haircut. A few decided not to try out just for that reason. Friends Rick, Charlie, and others, along with me, decided to do it. You remember more significant incidents more clearly. At one practice, I saw the runner and thought a great tackle was coming. Suddenly, out of nowhere, Glen blocked me; I was airborne and lay flat out while Coach Mr Owens came running over. "Are you alright there?" I caught my breath and said, "Yes." He said, "Okay, let's get up and continue." Glen was checking me, too. I told him, "Nice hit, and I will attempt to get you back even though you're bigger than me." He just smiled.

At that time, the drinking age was twenty-one. Around the 1960s and 1970s, many states lowered the drinking age to eighteen. In one class, I recall the teacher instructing us to debate the drinking age. About half the class thought it should be twenty-one, while the other half thought it should be eighteen. I was on the twenty-one-year-old side of the class because we thought they would be more responsible. We were concerned about anyone harming themselves or others. As the debate continued, a girl named Mary Ann and I kicked some thoughts back and forth (once I made up my mind, it could rarely be changed). Mary said to me, "Why is it that you can be drafted and die for your country, but you can't choose to drink?" For a rare moment, I was quiet. Then I got up, walked to the opposite side of the room, and sat down as many of team twenty-one looked on. "I am now on the other side," I stated.

Now, another event with Pop. He found a great deal on a pair of shoes. So, he decided he could buy two. He kept one and gave another to my Uncle William. One day, while wearing those shoes, he walked over to my house and walked right out of them. The soles fell right off, at least on one of them. He mumbled something in Italian and then told my mom. We all got a kick out of it. Uncle William laughed when he heard the story. By the way, his own shoes lasted for years.

I was fortunate to be able to choose many things throughout my life. My family's military history was so honorable that I could never burn my draft card. I never would, though many did in the 1970s. Though I was eligible for the draft (for a short period), I was privileged not to have witnessed war. There were a few chilling moments I have experienced in my life, but nothing comparable to war. I have always had, and still have, so much respect for those who serve in the military that it cannot be explained in words. The Vietnam War could fill a novel on why and how it was handled, but that was not the focus of this book. If it weren't for those who served, there's no way we could have the free life we have. I will not argue this with anyone.

Dad and Bill were working on a plumbing and heating job at Tweed, New Haven Airport, while I was checking out the place. My brother and I had an opportunity to fly on an airplane. This would be my first flight. I don't think Mom knew about this until afterward. Bill and I got onto this small Piper Cub. The pilot gladly took us up for a ride. I thought it was pretty cool seeing everything around us from so high up. After a short time, the pilot asked, "How's your stomach?" Bill and I said, "Okay." Then Bill questioned, "Why do you ask?" Then, suddenly, we did a nosedive. Yikes! It was nothing for the pilot, but it was our first flight. It became a first-flight memory.

Mr. Sturtze & Pop

Just before I got involved with the drum corps, a school friend, Scott, asked if I would like to go camping with his family. It was quite a different experience. We camped in tents, went to a beach, canoed, fished—all sorts of things. One night, a big storm hit, and Scott and I woke up soaked because the tent was leaking. So, we spent that night in the back of his dad's station wagon. Later, as I walked down the path to use the facilities, I fantasized about being in a big drum corps competition with thousands cheering. Even while I was camping, drumming was never far from my thoughts.

Our family liked animals, and dogs were among our favorites. However, growing up, we never had a dog in our house, as my mom had some allergies.

A few Saturday mornings were one of the only times Dad would get to sleep in. That's when a neighbor's two basset hounds decided to bark and howl. I could hear Dad saying, "Oh my God, oh my God, oh my God, the only morning I get to sleep in… Oh my God." Poor Dad!

We spent many weekends at the Colonial Club in Oxford, Connecticut. What a blast! Dad did quite a bit of plumbing work there. Mom would relax by the pool, and I usually spent my time in the pool and at the snack bar across the field. I met a lot of friendly people. At one time, I invited my friend Gary. We spent some time in the kitchen while the chef made a great meal.

Many marching band kids would get ridiculed or stereotyped as weak or strange. Fortunately, I did not see this as much at the schools in Wallingford. While I appreciated the talent, that style never interested me. However, rock and jazz piqued my attention. Later, I learned about a military-like marching and music style that began to coalesce during World War I. The Veterans of Foreign Wars (VFW) and the American Legion (AL) sponsored numerous competitions in the 1960s for various drum and bugle corps.

The Drum Corps Associates (DCA) was formed in 1965, and the Drum Corps International (DCI) was formed in 1972. The DCA was for all ages, whereas DCI has an age limit of 21. The military marching style was more disciplined, formal, and stricter. Formations were kept rigid. Music was becoming more modern, but still had many traditional components. It's sometimes challenging to explain. However, if you saw a typical marching band and a marching drum corps, you would likely notice quite a difference. Both were often stereotyped.

On July 4th, 1970, Wallingford, Connecticut, had its tercentennial parade. My good friend John had joined the Yankee Peddlers Drum and Bugle Corps at a young age. I was intrigued when I saw them marching by with that military style of form and music (you may be able to catch this on YouTube). This stuck in my mind, and John asked if I was interested in joining. His dad would also speak of the drum corps, the DCA, the Connecticut Hurricanes, the Hawthorne Caballeros, the New York Skyliners, and others. After gathering more information and discussing this with Mom and Dad, I joined the Yankee Peddlers Drum and Bugle Corps at Post 45 in Meriden, Connecticut.

One of the things that attracted me was the more traditional rudimental drumming style—one of the cleanest types of drumming. In other words, if you listen carefully to this type of drumming, you will notice that the style is cleaner, smoother, and more exact. Of course, all styles have their unique attraction. For example, orchestral percussion is impressive, especially because many players excel at playing various percussion instruments and sight-read music so well. Jazz drumming is excellent because of its improvisations. Rock drumming with its modern beats and moving music.

This was about September 1970. This would be a great way to learn some rudimental basics and try that kind of military marching style. Fortunately, the dues were affordable.

I arrived on my first day at the Yankee Peddlers Drum and Bugle Corps rehearsal. After signing up and being introduced to many lovely people, I anxiously awaited my first lesson. This may have been a typical day for most, but I had no idea what I was about to get myself into—no idea. An older gentleman was giving instructions on this beat-up old drum pad. Having somewhere between five and seven years of playing experience (if you want to call it that), I thought I was good (but not in a cocky way). I received instructions for the essential drum rudiments and knew the basics well enough.

The instructor called on me. How hard can this rudimentary stuff be? He politely requested that I play the single-stroke roll (L-R-L-R-L-R, which should be equally separated smooth beats). Then he asked me to play flams (LR-RL-LR-RL). The first tap in each spot is a grace note or lower and is lightly played. There should be a distinctive click sound. Then he asked me to play the long roll (LLRRLLRRLLRR). When fast, these beats should be smooth, open, bouncing, and separated.

"You seem to have a natural talent and promise, but wow, that was dirty. I will have to start you all over from the beginning!" Ouch! I mean, pop my balloon! "But what do you mean?" I politely asked. Then he played the long roll. I'm getting goosebumps just thinking about it. I never, and I mean never, have heard a smoother, longer roll in my life. I knew I would have to listen to him and increase my practice time. I had to get clean before attempting anything else.

By the way, I learned he was Earl Sturtze, arguably the absolute best in the rudimental field. He had a real knack for instructing. Many of his students were champions, and his students' students were also champions.

So, this is where drumming really gets its start. Mr Sturtze would say that drumming was an art and a science. I gained much more appreciation for drumming as I became more and more involved, especially with the rudimental snare. I realized that drumming can simultaneously be an artistic and a highly athletic endeavor.

Through trial and error, it took many generations to form the essential drum rudiments, which help drummers perform much more efficiently. For those non-drummers, think of rudiments like a house's foundation. With a solid foundation, you can build on it whatever you want. If the foundation is weak, forget it. I'll repeat: if the foundation is weak, forget it!

For now, I would continue to use my first "drum kit," which consisted of my father's bar stools, some boxes, and old chairs. I would play all types of records on that small record player, focusing on rock and jazz. I sometimes pretended I was Ringo or Buddy Rich; the make-believe crowds would go wild.

It was somewhere around the 1970s, and I was a whopping fourteen years old, and I thought I knew everything about the universe. Some events stick in your mind...

Mom was concerned after receiving a phone call from Aunt Millie. My Uncle Ed had experienced a panic attack and ran out to a small shed, frozen in motion. But Aunt Millie's nursing training came in handy, and she calmed him down. This had never happened to Uncle Ed before, and we didn't know what triggered it. Later, we heard about an air show and possible Japanese Zeros and summarized that it may have triggered something from his WW2 experience on the Pacific islands. Unbelievable.

Michael H Fiondella Jr

While my story is intended to be primarily about good memories, remember…

I looked forward to getting more drum corps experience and playing football at Moran Junior High School. After a football game in October of 1970, I was excited to have made a good tackle, and I couldn't wait to get home to tell everyone. When I arrived at the house, I was curious why so many cars were parked there and down the street, but I didn't think much of it. As I walked inside, my father greeted me. "Guess what happened at the game, Dad?" But he instructed me to follow him, and we went straight into my room. "I've got to tell you something… Pop passed away." I got lightheaded, and either Dad or Uncle William held me up. Then I lay on my bed. It's all a blur from here. No words, really. A million thoughts and no thoughts. A million whys and no answers. A million sad feelings and no feelings. We hold on to our faith as best we can. So many situations cannot be explained by mere words. Our family would never be the same. Fortunately, we were a strong and loving unit, but it was all different now. But knowing Pop, he would not want us to be miserable. He was and still is a massive influence in my life.

Choosing Music

Pop wanted us to be happy and for me to continue my music lessons. And sure enough, things got a little better as time passed.

My brother Bill attended Lyman Hall High School in Wallingford, Connecticut, but now a new school was being built. Mark T. Sheehan High School, founded in 1971, is the one I would attend. The school was named in honor of a medical officer in WWI who practiced medicine in Wallingford and was known to never refuse service to anyone, including patients who could not afford the care.

We had voted on the school colors — maroon and gold — and our mascot was the Titan. Coincidentally, those colors represented a particular drum and bugle corps that soon became a massive part of my life. One day, we were all lined up in the gym for an inspection by the athletic director. I used to get a kick out of teachers asking students, "Is John your brother?" or "Is Judy your sister?" However, since my brother and I were years apart, luckily, I didn't run into that problem until…

Mr. Riccitelli (aka Mr Ric) came from Lyman Hall High and became the athletic director at Sheehan. Along with his discipline and athletic leadership, he was also a wonderful, caring person. He always wanted us to be busy. Do good things, and he cared for us. I later learned that he had quite a military history but had never really talked about it. He eventually got to me as we formed an inspection line. "Fiondella, Fiondella," then, in a stronger voice, he continued, "Do you have a brother, Bill!" I answered, "Yes, sir." He said, "Blue chip, bluuuuue chip if you're half like your brother, you'll be good by me!" I thought that was pretty cool. My brother played football at Lyman Hall High School and was good at it.

"What's goin' on here?" he'd echo frequently. If anyone started mischief, he would yell, "What's goin' on here?" then settle the problem. One day, as I passed the gym on my way to class, I overheard someone ask, "Did you hear about the kid on the roof we had to go after last week?" Which was quickly followed by Mr Ric's voice echoing in the hall. "What's he doin' on the roof here?"

The sports I liked at that time were football and swimming. Rick and I decided to join the swim team in my sophomore year. That was quite an experience. The new pool needed repair at one point, so we had to swim at the YMCA at an ungodly hour in the morning. Yuk. We had an excellent coach, Mr Green, who gave us great confidence and led us to win the state championship that first year at Sheehan High School. I was average and only scored two points all year, but I did well considering I had never been on a swim team before, and I learned a lot from our great coach. I also received tremendous support from my swim mates. I even earned the nickname Flash. Please do not get the wrong impression; this had nothing to do with my speed. After several false starts from many swimmers during practice, Coach Green enthusiastically mentioned that there would be no other false starts. I don't think I was ever guilty, but of course, after his warning, it was my cue. Yep, the next race, I false-started. He couldn't help himself, so he burst out with a laugh and shook his head. "Okay, Flash, get going and catch up."

Mr Green and I would sometimes play chess after school. However, as I became more interested and involved in drum and bugle corps, I explained to him that I wanted to pursue drumming. Therefore, I wouldn't have time to dedicate to swimming. While I was certainly no star, I had a lot of respect for him. He really improved my swimming, and I even received a lifesaving certificate. At one lifesaving class, we were brought to the deep end of the pool, and for lack of a better explanation, we would pair up and try to drown each other. I suppose we needed to experience the panic of someone we were attempting to save. I do not remember the name of the guy I was paired with. Still, we were both good swimmers and of a good size, but the rules were to keep each other underwater until one pinches the other, using some common sense along the way. So, we went at it. I had a pretty good pair of lungs and could get a good breath, so I kept him under the water with me for some time. Then, he pinched me. As we let go of each other, however, as I was nearing the surface, he pulled me under before I could get a breath, and now he was on top of me. Now, I was pushing and pinching, and Coach Green had to break us up and calm us down. We must have sounded like two first graders: You pinched me, no, you pinched me, no, you pinched me... Boy, I learned how to manage myself in the water. As the season ended, I thanked Coach Green for everything, and he wished me good luck.

There certainly are some Drum Corps memories that aren't directly related... It was either a competition or a parade for the Yankee Peddlers Drum and Bugle Corps when I caught a ride in the equipment truck. What a ride it turned out to be. On the highway, out of nowhere, the dang hood popped up, and we couldn't see a thing. I think Phil, the drum major, was driving at the time, and he pulled over to fix it. I was laughing hysterically. He (or the other Phil) said, "Man, it's not funny; we could have been killed." But I suppose I laugh in similar situations rather than freak out.

At a later event, we rode in a bus, and while Phil, the bugle player, was standing in the middle of the aisle, the bus quickly stopped. Phil then went airborne past where I was sitting. I didn't laugh at that one, although it seemed funny afterward, as he didn't get hurt. Wow, this stuff could be dangerous.

More Yankee adventures include Dave B, a good (and loud) soprano horn player. He would make a mistake, then turn his horn immediately around and look into the bell side to see what had happened. That always cracked me up. John would also do that at times. Another was this poor bass drummer who needed to get one accent at the beginning of a song, but, for some reason, didn't quite get it after maybe eight tries. Mr Sturtze rarely lost his patience, but after the eighth time, he grabbed the bass drumstick and showed the drummer where the beat should be. Holy moly.

I don't recall the exact year, but I remember the moment. I wished so hard for my first drum set. One Christmas, I woke up half-asleep, walked down the hallway, turned the corner, and in that tiny living room near the front door, I noticed a gold sparkle—my first drum set. What a huge surprise! All I can think of as I write this is how my parents did this. Dad and I created an area in the basement for my setup, where I jammed to records.

One of the first songs I practiced and played repeatedly was Spinning Wheel by the group Blood, Sweat & Tears. Mary, my buddy Rick's sister, got me interested in the Chicago group, which had a unique sound and rare talent among many of the day's musicians. Of course, I also started jamming to many rock and jazz albums. I must have had a million Buddy Rich albums!

At this point, it was becoming drum rudimental madness. Every Sunday, there was practice at Post 45 in Meriden, Connecticut, with the Yankee Peddlers Drum and Bugle Corps. We'd begin with the drums in one room on the first floor, the horns practiced on the second floor, and the color guard met in another room. Mr. Sturtze mentioned that the corps needed a snare drummer immediately. He thought I could be pushed along a little faster. I could not wait until I had my chance to play with the whole corps.

Here's a memorable event. At one particular rehearsal, my father walked into the drum practice room. As I was at that old beat-up drum pad taking my lesson, my father said,

"Earl?" Then Mr. Sturtze said, "Mike?" Dad said, "I thought your name sounded familiar!" Earl said, "Well, I'll be. I thought your son's name sounded familiar!"

At one point, Mr. Sturtze lived across the street from my dad. My mom, by the way, also lived on that same street. My dad remembered him practicing at times. He was also friends with my family, so I ended up with what would turn out to be my primary fantastic drum instructor and a longtime family friend.

Since Mr. Sturtze was a rudimental expert, I had to ask, "How long does it take to learn all the 26 Standard American Rudiments?" He said, "If you practice enough, you could become a good drummer in about three years." That sure seemed like a long time to me. I kept involved, became serious about learning, and started practicing regularly. Then, Dad and Mom discussed having Mr Sturtze give me private lessons. Mr. Sturtze mentioned that he thought I had great potential and would like to provide me with those private lessons. He said he could even give me lessons at home on his way to another corps he taught. His cost was more than fair for that time, and I was fortunate that Mom and Dad let those private lessons begin. This would be a huge game-changer.

My mom would always make coffee and a snack for him. What a fortunate arrangement. I do not want to appear biased, but Mr. Sturtze and I had a unique connection. Besides being my primary drum instructor, he was a great friend and influence, and a part of the family. On one occasion, he offered to give me a ride to a Yankee Peddlers practice. I remember saying, "I can't wait for my first parade and first individual snare drum competition." He smiled and said, "I thought the same thing years ago, over fifty years ago!" As I write this, I will say the same thing. I would also learn about traditional fife and drum song standards, such as Downfall of Paris. One of my favorites in the Yankee Peddlers was Under the Double Eagle March. I honestly ended up with one of the most outstanding instructors ever.

Some thoughts and a basic understanding of drumming, particularly regarding rudimental drumming, might be a good idea for those without a musical background.

Drumming or percussion basics consist of music reading and rudiments. It took many generations to develop a set of unique sticking patterns or rudiments. These patterns, when practiced correctly, can provide a tremendous amount of control and coordination. Remember the example of the foundation of a house. If the foundation is strong, you can build almost anything; if not, forget it. Many have changed, added to, or provided many approaches to this idea. However, the 26 Standard American Rudiments are the absolute basics of percussion. NARD (National Association of Rudimental Drummers) was developed in 1933 at the American Legion National Convention in Chicago and had a strong influence on the drumming community.

A few examples are the single-stroke roll (L-R-L-R-L-R); these should be equally separated, smooth beats. Flams (LR-RL-LR-RL): the first tap in each spot here are grace notes, which are more lightly played, usually two inches or lower. The second beat is higher and louder, and there should be a distinctive clicking sound when playing. The long roll (LLRRLLRRLLRR) should be equally separated smooth beats, with bouncing separated smooth beats when fast. Single paradiddle (LRLLRLRR), evenly spaced beats with the first and 5th beat accented and the remaining taps at about six inches. It is not critical which hand you start with, but some competitions have specific rules. In reality, the single-stroke roll, the long roll, and the flams are the big three. Some might say just the first two or even the long roll, but I firmly believe that the single-stroke, the long roll, and the flams, as Mr Sturtze taught me, are the big three. Anything and everything you ever attempt in drumming comes from those fundamentals. If you can play them correctly and smoothly, you have the potential to go crazy.

Another memory comes to mind during this teenage period.

My buddy Rick and I were relaxing on the couch watching Bugs Bunny on a Saturday morning. It was snowing hard, and my dad must have run into something problematic because he came home spent. I had left my boots on the small deck outside, so when Dad entered, he saw Rick and me relaxing, watching cartoons. He views the boots, then turns to me and says, "What are these?" So, Rick decided to answer for me and said, "They're boots!" Then Dad said, "I give up." He walked into the house and the other room. Then Rick said, "Well, I better get going; see you later, Mike," and yelled, "See ya, Mr. Fiondella." I said, "Now you're leaving after giving that answer! Thanks!"

Pieces of Dreams

My buddy John was a great soprano bugle player, and Rick was a great French horn player. Rick accompanied John and me in the Yankee Peddlers, and he ended up with something equivalent to a French horn: a mellophone bugle. One of the many friends at the Peddlers was tenor drummer Al C. He was always full of fun and as funny as anything. He once drove us to the (newly built) Meriden Square shopping mall in a winter storm, doing donuts in the new parking lot. I also met what would become another wonderful friend, Dave P, another exceptional soprano bugle player. Among many others, John, Rick, Dave, and I would become close friends, and we all really enjoyed the corps and its music. We became interested in the marching and maneuvering competition. Finally, after practicing for many months, including private lessons, I participated in my first stint at the St. Patrick's Day parade in Holyoke, Massachusetts. After learning all the songs, I remember that day clearly as it was my first snare drumming experience, and boy, was it cold. My hands were frozen. I did not expect that day to end quickly, but it did, and we survived. We would go on to play in numerous parades and compete in the Connecticut Fifers and Drummers Association (CF&DA). Finally, after nearly two years, I entered my first snare drum individual competition. Mr. Sturtze certainly prepared me as best as he could. That first time up, in that small room in that school, I walked up in front of the judge to run down a few rudiments and play a solo.

Running down a few rudiments or opening and closing a rudiment meant starting slowly, gradually speeding up to play as fast as you can (as Mr. Sturtze would say, speed would come naturally), then gradually slowing down again. This was supposed to take one-and-a-half minutes to speed up and then one-and-a-half minutes to slow back down for each rudiment. Then, the few-minute drum solo. This did take practice and getting used to. I was so nervous that my legs were shaking and vibrating. I could have played a tremendous first-place solo if I had attached my sticks to my knees. I was determined to conquer this fear since I really wanted to play. It would take a little time, but I would finally get there.

Another recalled memory is the house being painted white. Initially, we had a dark charcoal-like color, but Mom wanted a white house. I remember my dad, brother, and uncles painting many coats to make the home white. Mom got her wish!

My buddies and I became curious about the more extensive marching and maneuvering drum and bugle corps, including the styles of music, the disciplined marching, and the popular music played. It seemed challenging and interesting, so we had to give it a try.

Next Decision

Uncle William (an engineer at Pratt and Whitney for twenty-two years) lived just a street away. Later in life, he would influence my engineering career. One day, while visiting us, Dad, Uncle William, and I were talking around a table when some questions I had about my future came up. My uncle turned to me and said, "Take a good look at your father and take a good look at me; who do you want to look like when you get older him or me?" We all laughed.

He was also a WW2 vet (mentioned earlier) and a POW for several years. I remember hearing how nervous he was on his first business flight on a jet. The flight attendant noticed his apprehension and asked, "Are you okay, sir?" "I'm used to propeller aircraft; this is the first time on a jet engine aircraft." As my uncle's coworker listened curiously, she asked. "Well, sir, do you see those engines out that window? Well, those engines are made by Pratt and Whitney, who also makes engines for the military and produce important parts for the space program." My uncle replied, "Do you see those parts inside that engine? I was involved in their design."

On one particular visit, Dad and I went to Uncle William's house. I was reminded of how well they got along, even though Dad was in the Navy and Uncle William was in the Army, just like many of my other uncles. This brings to mind how much I loved their discussions during Army and Navy games. Anyway, it was a very hot summer day. He had taken what was one of the worst yards in the neighborhood and transformed it into a beautiful home and garden. I noticed a hose that was wrapped on a unique stand next to the window near the small dining room area in the backyard. This water was taken from a pump system he designed, and he created a brook running through the yard with a cleaver dam and pump system to control the main flow of water. In any case, I said, "Hey, Unc, what's with that hose next to the window?" He replied, "That's a system I designed and set up. It lowers the room temperature by approximately two degrees." My dad looked at him, then me, saying, "He's nuts." And as usual, we all laughed.

As time passed, I gained more confidence. After a few years in the Yankee Peddlers Drum and Bugle Corps, John, Rick, Dave, and I became interested in a more demanding style. I would win and lose a few snare drum competitions in the Connecticut Fifer and Drummer Association, which was and is a highly respected organization. Mr Sturtze's style was traditional, and his approach was unique. Hence, you needed a combination of physical, musical, and mental attributes.

We even made up a drill with music on our own time in a field next to Post 45. There's certainly nothing wrong with all these other corps. It's just that we craved a more competitive style. I remember an extraordinary gentleman named Frank, who became a good family friend and would take my friends and me to see the Connecticut Hurricanes Drum and Bugle Corps practice. He usually had a pipe and was familiar with the newer style.

In the 1960s and early 1970s, the senior drum and bugle corps was the best for marching music-type performances. There was just something about the military style, discipline, and strong sound. It's tricky to explain, but the accuracy and power were unreal and unmatched. I will never understand how the senior corps obtained its fantastic sound while many held full-time jobs and family commitments. Their dedication was outstanding. (I was uncertain about getting involved with the senior corps due to the commitment under those circumstances.)

As any corps member knows, it's the love for the music style. You do not get paid or receive endorsements and must sacrifice most of your spare time. It's not unusual to pay dues.

At the same time, some might ridicule or stereotype us. I watched a football game on TV when a well-known player criticized the marching band on national television—how arrogant and ignorant. On that same note, some years later, the famous quarterback Steve Young and his family watched a DCI West show, recognizing the tremendous hard work and talent.

The 1972 Connecticut Hurricanes Drum and Bugle Corps show was unique and incredible. If you listened, you would be impressed. They played Fanfare for the New, Fiddler on the Roof, Malaguena, The Impossible Dream, America the

Beautiful, Rule Britannia, La Marseillaise, Fanfare for the Common Man, Hang 'em High, The Magnificent Seven, and Sprach Zarathustra. What a show. It was spectacular.

The horns were guided mainly by Joe Genero, and the drums by Ray Luedee. The marching and color guard were also superb. This corps was known for many things, including "They Call the Wind Maria" and "Hang Em' High/Magnificent Seven. The crowd would go completely nuts when they heard those numbers.

The Fanfare Fresh Air Fanfare was a show sponsored by the Connecticut Hurricanes in Hamden, Connecticut. Seeing these corps for the first time really left a lasting impression on me. Eventually, John, Rick, Dave, and I decided to try this style. We asked if the Yankee Peddlers might try this type of competition compared to a standstill, but they voted against it. Some corps are not into that style or commitment. They did not want us to leave but were understanding. By then, I'd also been taking private lessons with Mr Sturtze. During one lesson, he handed over a vast selection of drum and bugle corps records, further fueling my drive.

These corps' sound and raw power differed from anything, comprising seventy or eighty horns, twenty-five drums, and twenty-three color guards. The unique military style, including flags and rifles spinning at incredible rates like fast propellers, was just mesmerizing. It gave me goosebumps. No electronics or amplification. Horn lines had their lungs, drums had their hands, and guards had arms and legs. That's it! Whatever you could carry and provide was it.

Pieces of Dreams

My buddies and I looked at several units in Connecticut, and there were quite a few. I visited the Golden Crusaders from Meriden, Connecticut. They were great and welcoming. I entered the door, and they immediately had me practicing the snare line. "I'm just visiting," I'd repeat. But I made several friends right away, especially Al. In any case, I just wanted to see a few corps before committing. One that got my attention was the Emerald Cadets from New Haven, Connecticut. I was impressed with their show. They were becoming one of Connecticut's best junior drum and bugle corps.

I remember hearing about a drummer in the Emerald Cadets named Jim, a Junior State snare champion in the CF&DA, who was a genuine, nice guy. Since he was one of Sturtze's student's students, I thought he might be the person to talk to. At one particular fife and drummers competition, Rick, John, Dave, and I heard he was there. I nervously approached him and said, "Excuse me, are you Jim, a snare drummer in the Emerald Cadets?" He looked at me, hesitated, then slowly looked everywhere on the field before exclaiming, "I must beeeeee!" We immediately all laughed, and that meet-and-greet always stayed in my mind. He gave us tons of information and became another great lifelong friend. By the way, I learned that my cousin Rich (another good horn player) was in the unit. The Emerald Cadets' story would begin...

That summer, we saw an Emerald Cadets practice at the Amity Shopping Plaza in New Haven, Connecticut, and hearing that Hall of the Mountain King 'Off the Line' (the first song) was fantastic. What a sound. I also remember hearing If I Ruled the World, Greensleeves, and Old Man

River. I loved the brass and percussion. The color guard was also impressive, with rifles spinning like propellers tossed into the air. Later that day, we told them we were joining in the fall. I believe Ray Luedee was the drum instructor that year; an incredible teacher and well-known in the corps world. To my knowledge, he had been a student of Earl Sturtze.

I continued practicing, spending as much time as possible working on rudiments and solos and collecting records, including tons of Buddy Rich, which I played repeatedly.

Back home, Mom was becoming more worried about her mom living alone. Mom and Dad asked me what I thought about the possibility of Grandma taking my room. Dad would build a downstairs 'apartment' for me. That would be a super idea. Grandma was highly reluctant since she thought she was kicking me out of my room. However, I told her I'd have my own area and explained how excited I was. Still, it took some convincing, but she finally agreed. I loved having her there because nothing compares to her wisdom and experience. She always saw the good in people and was always so gracious.

Around this period, my dad and I heard that Buddy Rich would perform at the Holiday Inn Hotel in Meriden, Connecticut, right off Route 91. He asked if I wanted to see him. An easy answer: yes! We arrived and entered the room. The band was absolutely fantastic. They played many numbers I knew and had heard from my records many times. When they took a break, my dad said, "Let's try to meet him." I was so overwhelmed and hesitant. Wow, I should have done it. What a great band, and an absolutely incredible drummer to watch—definitely one of the greatest ever.

Believe it or not, I'm not usually a fan of drum solos! If drums overpower a song, it destroys it. It's smooth and natural when I hear Buddy Rich and others do a drum break.

Mom, Grandma, and I were waiting for Dad and Bill to arrive home for dinner. But when we saw them, Dad seemed out of sorts. It was then that we noticed stitches on his face and head. "Are you alright? You look a little funny," Mom said. "Ya, I got buried alive at work," he said calmly. "I'm kind of tired, so I'm going to lie down for a while." Then he walked to the bedroom as if it were just another day.

What's it with these WW2 vets? We were all stunned and sat there in silence. After a pause, my brother Bill explained that when Dad was handed a cast-iron pipe to place into a lower ditch, the sides suddenly caved in, trapping him. However, the pipe became a tool to help him breathe—what a clever reaction! My brother then yelled for the backhoe. Then, all the workers used their bare hands to dig the rest of the way. Then, he went to the hospital for several stitches. At least this had a good ending.

It makes me recall a story when he was in the Navy on that small destroyer. During one massive storm, he almost got washed overboard, but a few sailors helped him back up on deck as he clung for dear life onto ropes. My dad had at least nine lives, if not more.

The National Association of Rudimental Drummers emphasized the importance of sticking patterns for drumming to develop coordination. This approach helps drummers or percussionists establish a rhythmical structure. Finally, in February 1973, I received a vital certificate (a milestone for me) from NARD via Mr Sturtze. I was just as proud to receive it from NARD as I was to have Mr Sturtze as the examining judge.

Around this time, I also received the Sturtze School of Drumming Certificate for Rudimental Drumming. This might be of no significance to many, but for rudimental drummers, it really meant something.

On another note, occasionally, Dad would sing some songs as they came on the radio, especially Nat King Cole's The Christmas Song. Every time I hear it, it takes me back. I always thought Nat King Cole had one of the greatest natural voices ever. I should mention that Dad didn't sound half bad singing it, too.

Emerald Cadets

Dad and Mom supported my music; deep down, I have always appreciated it. Dad would remind me that even though I chose music, I needed to make a living. I gave this much thought, and he was right. This does not mean you should give up on the things you love, but we all need a foundation.

After many years of wanting a Cadillac, my dad finally purchased a used red Cadillac Eldorado. I was finally old enough to obtain a driver's license.

It was an extremely hot summer day, and the tester, a pleasant middle-aged guy, appeared exhausted and sweating. But when he got into the air-conditioned Eldorado, he sat back like he was going on vacation. After the test, he paused, turned to me, and said, "Okay, go in and get your license." An exciting moment in the life of a teenager.

After John received his license, he drove us to church. We had plans to go somewhere right after mass, but as we approached his car, we noticed he had a flat tire. His dad happened to drive up next to us, stopped, opened his window, and said, "Don't worry; it's only flat on the bottom." Then he left. Another jokester like my dad.

In September 1972, Rick, John, Dave, and I joined the Emerald Cadets Drum and Bugle Corps, which Father Mitchell directed. The corps usually met at Assumption Church in Woodbridge, Connecticut, on Tuesdays (for music) and at the New Haven Armory on Thursdays (for drill). We often practiced at the Amity Shopping Plaza parking lot during the summer.

We were nervous, but it helped that my cousin Rich and my good friend Jim (state champion) were there to ease our pain. Charlie Poole was the instructor with an impressive and incredible reputation as a champion snare drummer and performer. I was given a snare drum and sticks and put in the snare line. Jim had previously familiarized me somewhat with what to expect. Still, with little experience, I initially struggled. Charlie was strict but also compassionate, guiding me along. Eventually, with determination, I caught on and became more comfortable. Many things I never imagined were about to begin...

On Tuesday evenings, the unit would begin by cleaning and shining our instruments. Then, we'd line up for inspection. The more experienced drummers would show us tricks to clean between the drum head and the rim, using a small piece of cardboard or something similar to hold the drum head in place. Pepe (another great instructor) often made us laugh, but we always tried to maintain our military bearing during inspection. If he spotted a small piece of dirt, he would suddenly yell, "What's dis? Clean it up!" You could hear quite an echo while sticking his head into one of the large horns. We found it quite hilarious.

Some weeks passed, and when Rick, John, Dave, and I arrived at practice, there was talk about members trying to form a larger corps with other drum corps members in Connecticut. After all the preparation and excitement, we finally gained ground and didn't know what to think. This would suddenly become a challenging and rebuilding year for Emerald during the 1973 season. After some settling and changes, we ended up with a well-known, established instructing staff in the drum corps, including John Bodnar for the drums, Joe Gennaro for the horns, Carman Cluna for marching & Pepe Nataro for the horns and marching. Our show repertoire was Warsaw Concerto, Greensleeves, Old Man River, Spring Is Here, In the Good Old Summertime, Autumn Leaves, The Christmas Song, Auld Lang Syne, and Our Love. Week by week, practice after practice, we gradually improved. We really worked at the show. We all wanted to bring Emerald back to an excellent competitive position.

Uniquely, we had three sets of identical twins. Dave was the drum major, and Larry was the horn player. Patty and Mary were in the guard, and there were two other talented brothers, but I won't include them because I don't want to misspell their names.

In the 1970s, judging the marching and maneuvering style of drum and bugle corps relied heavily on the "tick" system (one-tenth point deduction), where execution was a huge part of the scoring. Drum and bugle corps roughly consisted of 128 members, with an average age of fourteen and a maximum of twenty-one. For example, there could be eighty horns, twenty-five drums, and twenty-three color guard members.

Judging relied on straight lines, military bearing, and execution; we were docked points for any errors. Music had to be clean; i.e., the snare line needed to sound like one person. The stick heights had to be identical. This included visually having the drumsticks in the same motion and height mirror images from person to person. Horns needed to hit their notes precisely, and the guard needed to be in sync, which included rifle twirling.

 The intense raw power and clean-sounding brass with the drums or percussion sound is difficult to explain. It was like a big rock band or jazz band on foot. Repertoires began to include many styles, such as rock, jazz, and classical. However, the choice of music never took away from the military's strict marching style and precision. There were undoubtedly great senior and junior drum and bugle corps in the early years, including the 1960s. Still, in the 1970s, drum and bugle corps would take off. It would take considerable time and sacrifice for the corps to be recognized for their unique talent, athletic ability, and raw power, leading to an exponential increase in practice times.

Weeks passed as we continued learning parts, and the instructional staff settled in and changed. Mr Cluna had us study and memorize names of formations and practice each over and over and over, such as what a squad was (a small number of individuals for drill), a platoon (a subdivision of individuals), or an oblique turn (marching at an angle) or dress (align with the person to the side). We usually used the New Haven, Connecticut, armory on Thursdays during the cold season indoors, repeatedly going over these marching maneuvers.

We were helped in smaller groups to learn the basics. Then we would all line up, the drums, the horns, and the guard without instruments. He'd yell, "Corps, attention." Now, standing perfectly still and upright with correct posture, chin up, shoulders back, and stomach in. He would inspect us later on. Then he would yell, "Mark time, march." Starting with the left foot and high leg lift, typically where our thighs were somewhat parallel to the ground, we adjusted the leg lift heights to ensure uniformity between tall and shorter members. In drills, we would be positioned to be as uniform as possible. We would be taught to dress correctly, visualize the person's appearance, and maintain a straight line as we march.

I believe the Casper Troopers of Casper, Wyoming, were some of the best marchers ever. Keeping a straight line takes a lot of energy, work, and practice. Then Mr Cluna would say, "Forward march." Our massive company front moved through the armory, trying to stay straight. I remember Pepe yelling several times in a funny (but still serious) tone, "You people are not dressed, you people are not in step, you people are causing your own prooooblems!"

Pepe was such an excellent, joyous, and knowledgeable instructor. Here's another moment... During one rehearsal, Pepe approached me (remember I was a newbie) and handed me his wet, yucky cigar. "Drummer, hold dis." So, I did. My buddies and I also wondered how long I was supposed to do this. Later, I approached Pepe and asked, "Mr Notaro, what would you like me to do with this? Do you want it back?" "I don't know, throw it away or something." It was a good laugh for him and my buddies.

Many days and years would pass quickly. My brother lived next door to Jack Libro, who owned Goldie and Libro's Music Center in New Haven, Connecticut. Dad and Bill unknowingly discussed getting me a chrome snare drum. One day, while visiting Jack's home, he had me play a new chrome (much heavier, I should mention) marching snare. Wow, what a great surprise. Jack helped me tremendously and was a great friend and supporter, constantly calling me Junior.

I always remembered Buddy Rich's white pearl-like drum set. I asked Jack to look for a set. A new set was out of the question, but I would put money aside. Of course, living at home at the time made that much easier. But I never imagined it would happen.

Eventually, I received a phone call from Jack. The conversation went something like this... "Junior! It's Jack. I might have something you're interested in. A guy with lots of money purchased a Rogers white pearl drum set about a week ago, but he got bored after playing it for a week. Would you like it for a few hundred bucks? We could discuss it, but I don't think they'll be available for long. What do you think?" Well, of course, I said yes! Now I had white pearl Rogers. Man!

More weeks passed. Emerald Cadets' repertoire for the 1973 season was the Warsaw Concerto, Greensleeves, Old

Man River, Spring Is Here, In the Good Old Summertime, Autumn Leaves, The Christmas Song, Auld Lang Syne, and Our Love. From memory and pictures, the snare line was Lynn, me, Jim, Melvin, and Kenny. Ron was also seen in some pics of the snare line, possibly later, and I was excited to be a part of it. There were many great members, including, but not limited to, my cousin Rich, Keith G, Dee Dee, Gail D, Mary, and the Patty twins. We had one guy nicknamed Rockin' Eddie. He was such a gentle soul. He may have been autistic. He had so much heart, cared for the corps, and helped tirelessly with the equipment. He would set us back on the right path if the buses got lost. Some bystanders gave him a difficult time at one show, and when we heard about it, we immediately stopped it.

Several contests and practices occurred during the year, and we had ups and downs. There were lots of get-togethers, parties, practice, and fun. Seeing and hearing larger crowds, often thousands of people, was so rewarding. When the corps had a good day, the crowd responded loudly, which brought a feeling that was difficult to explain. Many in the crowd would tell me they got goosebumps, and we would, too. The giant roar of many thousands was undoubtedly a thrilling experience.

We talked about significant contests, like the World Open in Massachusetts, the US Open Championships in Ohio, and a newly formed Drum Corps International (DCI) association, which held its first official competition in 1972. Many associations, like the American Legion and VFW, were some of the main sponsors of competing Drum Corps. Still, eventually, DCI started to organize more significant competitions. This activity was about to explode. In many ways, we were among the pioneers of the drum and bugle corps in the modern age. It was exciting, but I hoped that not all traditions would be lost. I liked the traditional approach with a contemporary twist.

Sixteen and Onward

At sixteen, a lot more was about to change. My buddies and I could now drive to places, including drum corps practices. We really watched out for each other and took care of each other. While I attempt to remember all the names and events, it's impossible. I'm trying. Rick, John, Dave, Louie, and Jim come to mind. Rick, John, and I lived on the same streetcar path and pooled our money, but one day, Rick and I had our parents' old cars and drove separately. On Route 15 North on the way home that night, I was in front and noticed him passing me, so I sped up; then he sped up, then… Soon, his car began to shake. The cars were doing the dancing-shaking thing—the twist on steroids. No worries, nothing illegal here. Finally, we backed off. It didn't really matter who ended up first.

Dad and Mom discussed that I should get a job. I'd have to start working for a living (was this a hint?). I was already used to doing chores, which included taking care of my parents and Grandma's yard and shoveling the two driveways in the winter. In reality, I knew I was fortunate. I worked with Dad at his plumbing and heating business for a bit. They really knew their stuff, and I learned a little from them. I recall learning how to solder copper piping and how to place cast iron pipes with molten lead. It was a hot summer day, and my brother was below in a ditch, connecting two cast-iron pipes. Sweat was pouring off his head. As he cut the excess piece, he threw it to me, saying, "Do you really want to do this for the rest of your life?"

I liked working with my hands and being outside, but it made me think about long-term work, and I was fortunate to have choices. I was taught that no matter what job you have, whether you like it or not, you must do it well. After all, someone is paying you to do some task. For the most part, if you disliked a job, you could always change it.

An outstanding, innovative, and friendly neighbor, as well as a great family friend, Gregg Cocco had an electronics business. He and Dad were good friends and worked together on occasion. Dad was also a good friend of Ben Segal, co-owner (with Bob Hall) of the Oakdale Musical Theatre in Wallingford, Connecticut, founded in 1954. Dad and Gregg also worked at the theatre. I ended up with a summer job helping Gregg.

I really took an interest in electronics and learned so much from Gregg. He would be one of the most significant influences in my electrical engineering career. Gregg would become the audio engineer for Oakdale Theatre, which changed from a tent theatre in the round to a dome theatre in 1972. I assisted Gregg and his crew in installing a new, state-of-the-art audio system in the theatre. What an exciting job!

As an aside, Dad would meet many stars and take pictures with them, including Jay Leno and Don Rickles.

Pieces of Dreams

I worked there on and off for several summers and did almost everything. I worked on the parking crew, stage crew, maintenance crew, gates, and the box office. Ben Segal's son, Beau, and daughter, Rebecca, were kind, hard workers, and good friends.

I was working the gates one night and was told not to let anyone inside unless they had a ticket. When a kind gentleman approached the gate, I politely blocked his way and asked, "Do you have a ticket, sir?" "But I'm Bob Hall." I said, "Sorry, sir, I can't let you in without a ticket." I had never met Bob before, so I had no idea who he was. Soon, Ben approached the gate with my dad. "He's okay, he's with us," they laughed. "I guess you know who Bob is now," Dad quipped. Oops! How embarrassing, but I was doing my job!

Speaking of Oakdale Theatre, I recall The Ink Spots, an incredible singing sensation. I was young, and I remember my dad inviting them over for spaghetti dinner when they performed at the Oakdale Theatre. I believe the bass singer loved my mom's spaghetti and looked forward to it whenever he was in Wallingford. What a happy, talented, and friendly guy. He was always so thankful for that dinner.

Are you asking about the Tom Jones show? Well, there are some interesting moments. I was one of many young guys chosen to guard him during his performance. I was in the front row in one of the aisles between the two sides, blocking anyone from running onto the stage. Along with the screaming crowd, one young girl was smirking in front of me. "You're loving this, aren't you?" she smirked. "I'm just doing what I'm told," I said.

I recall Peggy Fleming at Oakdale and the temporary ice rink for that performance. What a day and night that was. Setting up and removing the ice rink in the middle of the theater was labor-intensive and tough. I wouldn't want to do that again.

I was right next to the stage during the show, handing performers microphones. Peggy happened to get a microphone from the other side of the stage. When it cut out, I raised my hand, and she grabbed a new mic. It was a cool moment.

Another unique moment was when a rock pianist performed; sadly, I can't recall his name. I do remember him playing an incredible version of MacArthur Park. He even played the part, hitting the strings inside the piano like a guitar. That always stuck in my mind. I was lucky to have a part-time music-related job and witness so much talent.

Even though I can't remember his name, I will never forget the kind police guard who often chatted with me while I worked the gate. But those memories still pop into my head. Specific phrases or statements stick with you, including when an older woman slowly entered the gate. After she crossed, I turned to the guard and said, "Maybe I don't want to get old?" He said, "Don't knock it; you might not make it." Ah!

Gregg Cocco invited me to his house to listen to his audio system, a Macintosh tube amplifier from the 1970s. How can I explain the sound? To this day, I have never heard a better system. Not even close! The sound was immaculate. He played some rock and jazz, and I could hear every singer's breath and every string on the guitars. Then he played a few drum and bugle corps albums and could distinguish each footstep. It was impressive and unreal. Luckily, he let me borrow one of those amps, and I've heard nothing that compares to it since.

I helped raise money for our corps during my time with the corps. We sold items to pay for equipment, buses, and other necessities. During one venture, we encountered a problem with a group of smart alecks. But as soon as word got around, Emerald formed a semi-circle near them and blew them away with songs ringing at 120 dB or more. That was cool. There's more than one way to take someone down.

On another evening at Amity Shopping Plaza, Rich (a friendly member) walked over to grab a bite. As he exited the restaurant, a gang of kids encircled him, not allowing him to pass. Someone alerted the corps, and over 100 encircled the gang of about fifteen. It was a different situation now. My cousin, a martial arts expert, along with others, was pushed to the front of the line. One of the bullies pulled a crowbar out of a trunk while my cousin moved closer. Fortunately, only words were exchanged, but thank God, nothing happened. They returned to their cars and drove erratically through our ranks, but the police ended it.

Dad, Mom, Grandma, and I were having a pleasant spaghetti dinner (perfect sauce or gravy, depending on where your ancestors hailed) when Dad quietly got up and went to the bathroom. He took longer than usual when Mom asked me to check on him. I knocked at the door and asked, "Dad, are you okay in there?" "Ya, ya, go eat. I'll be right there." Soon, he returned and began eating again. "What took you so long?" "My darn tooth was bothering me, so I pulled it." "What! With what?" "Ah, I used my plumbing pliers; why should I pay a dentist fifty bucks or more?" I said, "Yikes! You could get an infection!" "Nah, I dipped the pliers in alcohol; don't worry about it, and eat your dinner!" The WW2 generation again. Grandma remained silent, Mom shrugged, and I gave up. By the way, I go to the dentist; I don't have any at-home remedies.

One day, as we were all relaxing and watching something on TV, Dad was in pain—we could tell by the sounds he was making. Then, Mom, Grandma, and I noticed his big toe cramping at a ninety-degree angle, straight up. I have never seen anything like it. When it finally relaxed, we all laughed like crazy. Why does it seem hilarious when something happens to dads, but when it happens to our moms...

Here's another 'poor dad' event. Through the years, Bill has learned much from my father, and, in turn, I have learned from them. Sons will be sons. Bill was under the work truck in Grandma's driveway, making a repair. Dad kept telling Bill how to do the job and repeatedly instructed my brother. "Dad, why don't you go into the house and get a 'such and such' tool?" "What do you need that for?" Bill cooked up an answer. So, Dad headed into the house.

Meanwhile, my big brother Bill rolled out from underneath the truck, looked at me, and said, "He'll never find that tool. That ought a get rid of em' for a while." Then Bill rolled back under the truck. Later, when Dad returned, we all had a good laugh.

Since Jim and I were initially from the CF&DA, we still attended and enjoyed those competitions. Since the 1940s or 1950s, the CF&DA began having musters (get-togethers to play and have fun). At one point, there were even drummers from Switzerland (who had their own drumming style), and we became friends with a group. Not knowing the language, we laughed and joked in various ways. At one point, everyone took turns drumming parts. They would play something, and then Jim and I would join in. Then, it turned into a fun kind of competition. They played something more complex, and then we'd accept the challenge. Jim might yell something like, "You guys are nutty," and we'd all laugh. To this day, we probably had no idea what the others said, but it didn't make a difference. It was a blast.

Then Jim and I played a problematic phrase with fast singles with our left hand. A few of them looked at each other, and then one motioned to us with his drumstick (Uh, I want to keep this story rated PG, so use your imagination). We all laughed hysterically. Some things are universal. People everywhere have so much in common when it comes down to it. We traded some items, and I still have that shirt.

Frank Arsenault spoke with Jim and me after that fun moment with the Swiss drummers. He was an internationally renowned percussionist and teacher, famous for his marching percussion works. Earl Sturtze also taught him. He said, "It's amazing what guys are playing nowadays; great job." Jim and I were so appreciative. I said, "If it weren't for people like you, we would have never had this opportunity, and moments like this would have never happened; you're a legend and an incredible drummer." Frank was so friendly and modest.

I did attempt to compete in the CF&DA as an Emerald Cadet. I know this was a challenge since I was now in another organization. Still, as a Sturtze student, I also enjoyed the individual competition experience and thought I could learn more. As I became more comfortable, I tried a few more snare competitions, but this was usually not allowed. I realized I might be disadvantaged now that I was out of the CF&DA. However, the two richly talented guys respected my decision. One was Bill, and the other was Keith, a junior Connecticut State Champion. I really wanted to win over Keith since he was the Connecticut Champ, and I could no longer officially compete for that state title.

After losing to Keith, some of Emerald's staff suggested I might not want to compete in another organization. Still, they left the choice up to me. However, I kept on trying, and I finally won. What a great feeling. I congratulated Keith several times on his win, and he was gracious in return. "That only took a million times," and we laughed.

One day, as I walked into class, I noticed something unusual. Bill had both wrists in a cast. "I was doing a long jump, fell backward and landed wrong, and broke both my wrists," he admitted. "Wow, I look forward to you getting better soon. Knowing you, it will only be a matter of time before you start drumming again." What were the chances of something like that happening? In addition to competitions, a few drumming duets with Dee Dee provided silver and gold medals. I still don't know how she and others carried those heavy triple drums. I always thought that the Emerald Cadets were a very talented corps. I believe you would agree if you heard any of their recordings. Sometimes, you need a little more than talent to play with the big guys.

If you're interested in hearing classic drum and bugle corps, check out YouTube. You'll see and hear the professionalism. Think of Olympic athletes as an analogy. Future studies would find that the athletic ability of the drum and bugle corps members was just as impressive and challenging as that of athletes in traditional competitions.

Mary and William Giordano
(Mom's parents)

Almerinda and Ciro Fiondella
(Dad's parents)

Giordano Bros Monumental Work

Mom

Dad

Mr. & Mrs. William D. Giordano

request the honour of your presence at the

marriage ceremony of their daughter

Rosaline Amelia

to

Michael Harry Fiondella

Monday morning, September the first

Nineteen hundred and forty-one

nine o'clock

St. Ann's Church

Hamden, Connecticut

RECEPTION: 3 - 6 P.M.
COLONIAL HOUSE
2389 DIXWELL AVE.

Mom and Dad's Wedding Invitation

Mom and Dad's Wedding Party

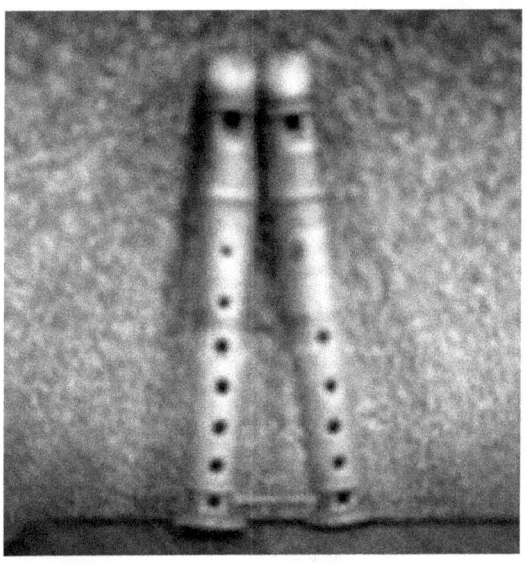

Great Grandfather Michael Fiondella's double flute

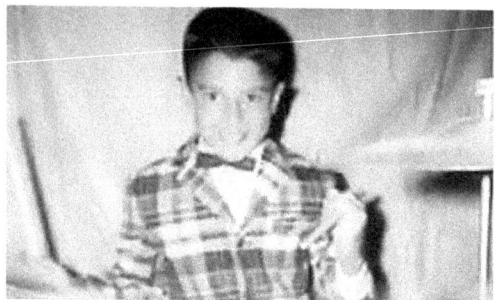
Yours Truly first drum set lesson

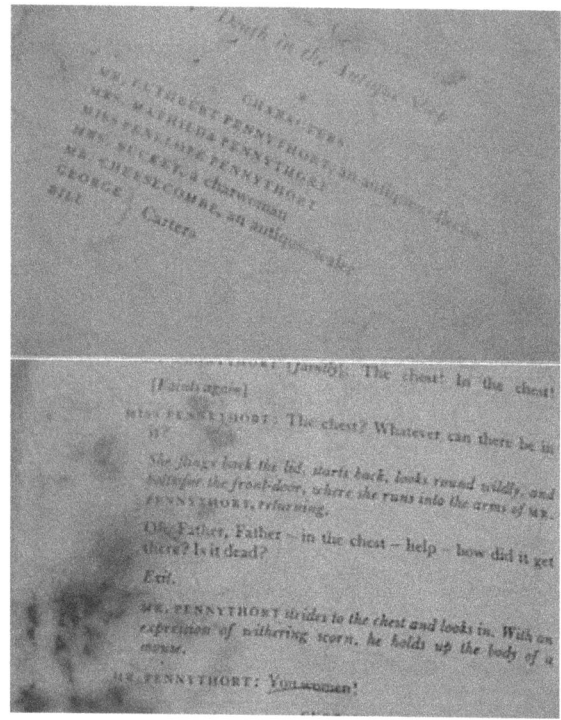
Death in the Antique Shop 6th grade play

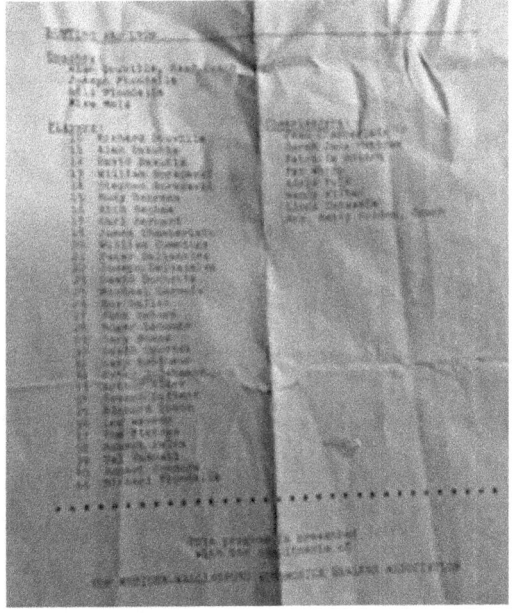

Football team in younger years

The tape recorder

The infamous Flexible Flyer sled

A family photo

Moran Junior High School's football award

American Legion Post 45

Some basic drum rudiments

Single Stroke Roll

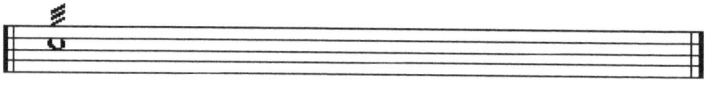

Long Roll

Single Paradiddle

Single Ratamacue

Flams

Flamaccent

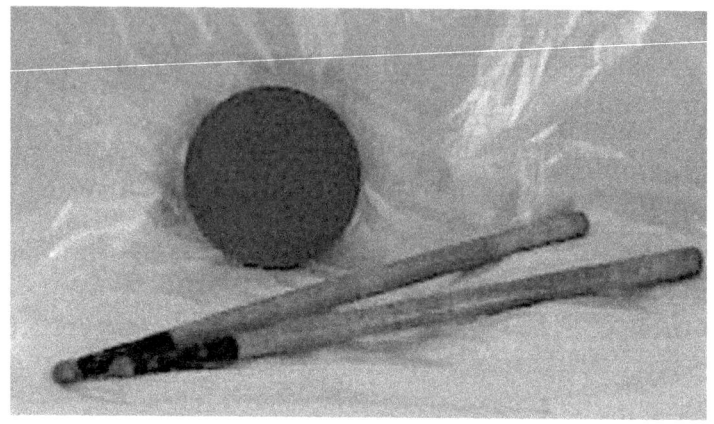

First drumsticks and pad

First drum kit

First lesson with Mr Sturtze

Me as a Yankee Peddler

Mr Sturtze, Mom, a friend and Uncle William - circa 1940s

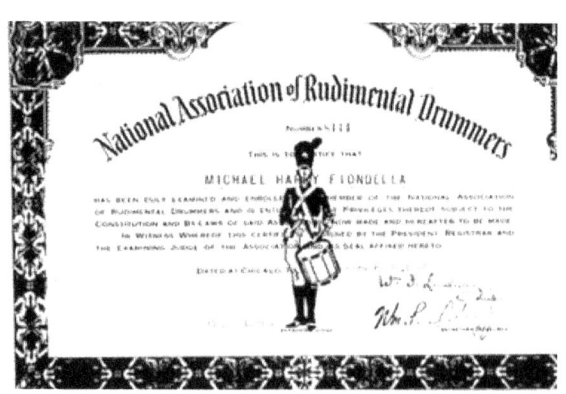

Me on drums, John, nephew Jay on bongos, Rick

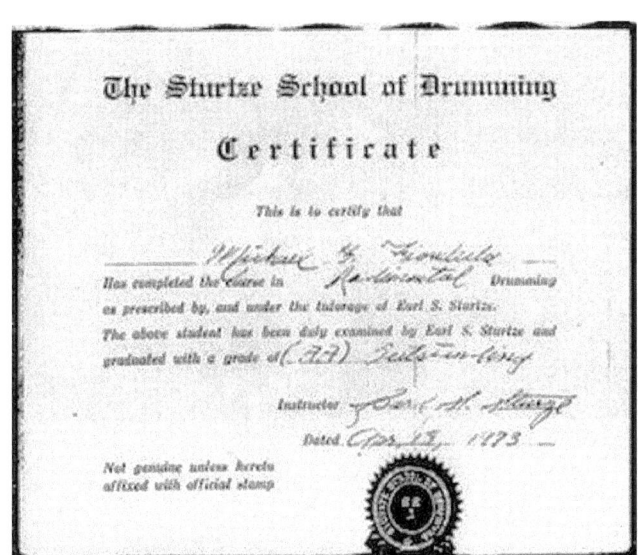

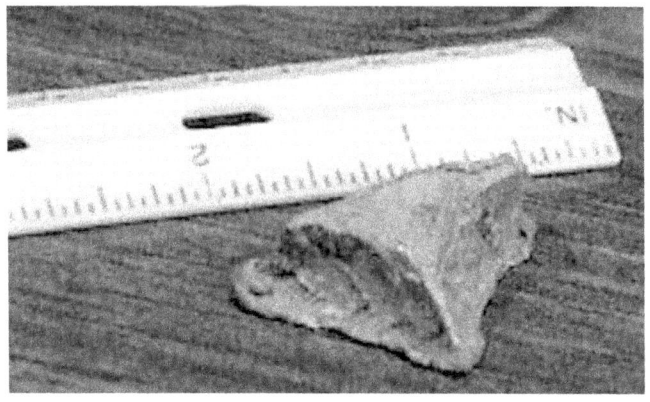

Piece of lead from my brother's job

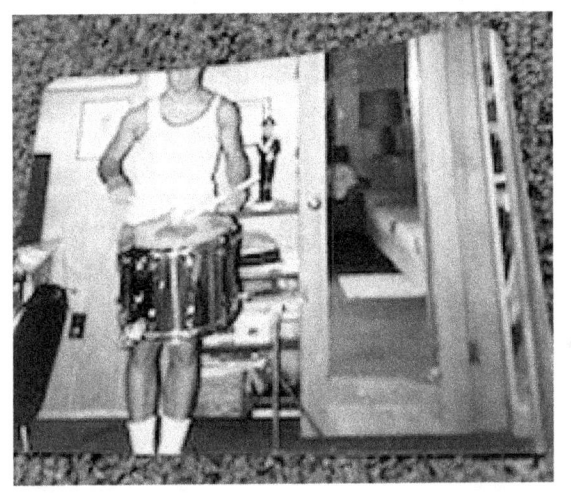

Yours Truly, well most of me!

Last lesson with Mr. Sturtze

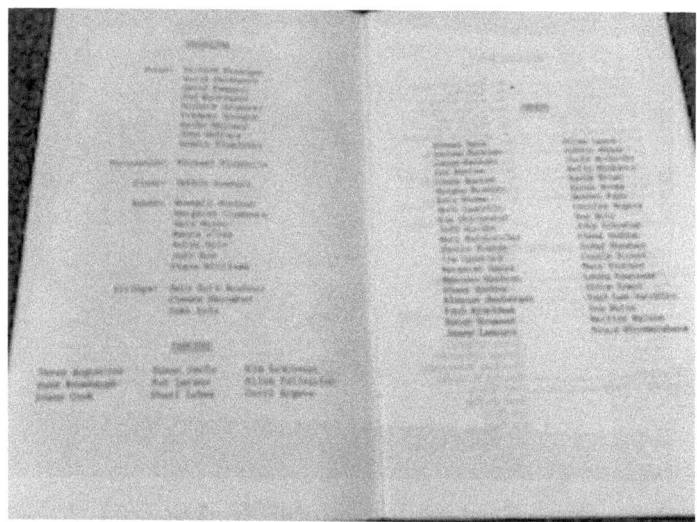

Funny Girl play in high school

Yours Truly at Citadel

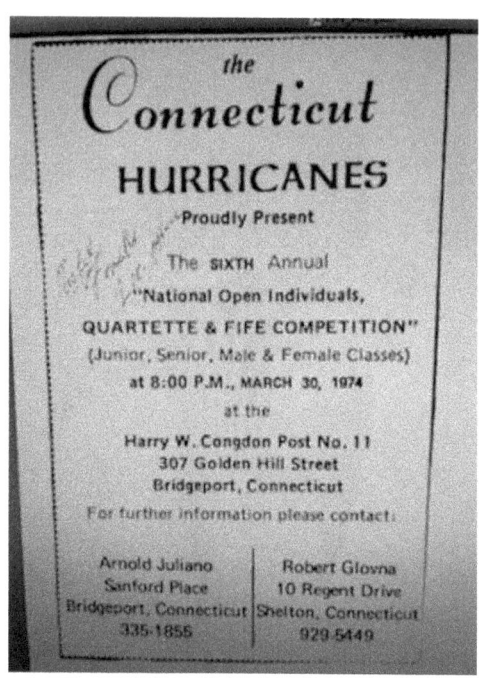

Hurricanes Nationals 1974

DCI patch and necklace

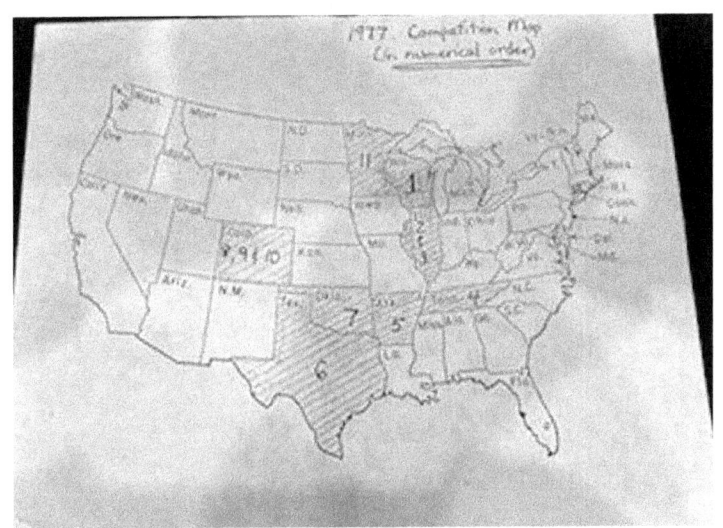

Garfield Cadets 1977 DCI Tour Map

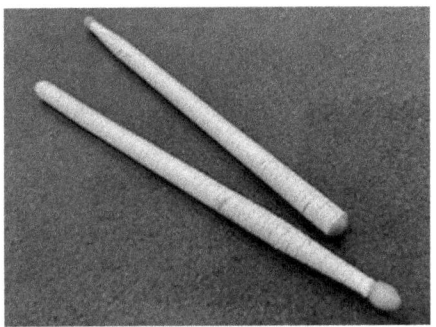

Garfield Cadets drumsticks 1977

Michael H Fiondella Jr

Competition Time

My experiences in drum and bugle corps competitions increased, and I also began to compete more in individual snare drum competitions. By the latter part of the 1973 season, Emerald really improved, and there was also talk of the US Open Championships in Ohio and the World Open in Massachusetts. I was curious about the shows with larger crowds, and Jim would try to explain his experiences from 1972. As DCI gained popularity, many of the best corps of the time also began to join that association.

Little did I know at that time that some very special and wonderful people would be watching us rehearse—my future wife and her family. Small world.

Emerald was more of a competitive corps, but we also participated in parades and halftime shows for financial assistance. We did one exhibition at Yankee Stadium, and since most of my family were Yankee fans, it made it more special. In any case, we were playing when the sprinkler system turned on. Ah, an unforgettable moment. As far as that Yankee game, Dave, I, and many others talked about witnessing one of Greg Nettles's greatest games.

I distinctly remember a recording from a particular show with the scoring results. "In 6th place with a score of 45.75, the Buccaneers. In 5th place, with a score of 47.95, the Vanguard. In 4th place with a score of 62.15, the Golden Crusaders. In 3rd place with a score of 67.70, the Stateliners." This was followed by various levels of cheering. "In 2nd place with a score of 68.55, the Surfers", with screams from many, including my dad and Rick's mom. And we know by now… "1st place with a score of 71.75, The Emerald Cadets." The crowd went wild! I'll never forget that feeling. Then we played the Warsaw Concerto while exiting the stadium. You could then hear people yelling, along with my dad and Rick's mom laughing joyfully.

My house was next to a thickly wooded area with a large farm field. Next to that field was Masonic Home, a care facility. One day, I was outside and heard a unique set of brass chords and cool-sounding Latin music in the distance. It ended up being the Hawthorne Muchachos, a fantastic junior drum and bugle corps. What a phenomenal sound. They used to stop at the facility to perform.

As everything continued, Mom and Grandma did an incredible amount of work around the house and everywhere, helping anyone they could whenever they could, all while keeping us fed and happy. I received compliments constantly from friends and family alike. I was highly active, and I know I ate like a horse. Dad used to say he might need to get a second job, although he was always so busy working his butt off as it was. I was sitting with Grandma one day and heard some terrible news. What a shock. "Grandma, I don't understand why countries cannot get along better." She replied in her usual calm manner, "Michael, some families and neighborhoods can't get along; how are countries supposed to?" She also said, "Remember, always keep God in front of your eyes."

Jim would mention the larger crowd sizes for shows like the World Open and the US Open for Drum and Bugle Corps. As DCI gained ground, some groups would still participate in other contests. After rebuilding, all the Emerald Cadets hoped we could still make one or some of these finals. We were getting closer to the World Open preliminaries. There would be about thirty-one corps attempting to make it into the top ten to perform in the final competition.

There were a few smaller shows worth noting before the World Open. My brother visited the New Haven area to watch us perform with his family. I remember two main events. It ended up pouring, and I mean, it was torrential rain. My poor brother and family got soaked, as we all did.

In the middle of the show, I noticed a drumstick go airborne and land in the wet ground, sticking straight out. Then I heard Jim. "My goodness gracious, I think I lost my stick." It was good that none of the drum judges witnessed him talking, but a judge ran to retrieve it for Jim. I did everything I could to not burst out laughing and maintain my military composure. Regardless of what happens, you must always remain silent and composed.

One routine required facing each other and striking the other person's sticks (fencing). During one show, as I turned to face Jim, a strange look appeared on his face. Think of it like a cartoon character who got hit over the head with a huge cooking pan. Then, the poor guy collapsed like a rock. As I mentioned earlier, we were instructed to continue playing as if nothing had happened. Still, the medical staff were always on standby. My instinct was to stop and help, but I couldn't. After the show, we ran to see how he was. "Jim, are you okay?" "My goodness gracious, I must have fainted!" he stated, cool as a cucumber. We just laughed.

As we were lined up, preparing to start, the announcer would say, "Are the judges ready?" They'd reply with a wave or salute, then say, "Emerald Cadets, is your corps ready?" Then, the drum major, Dave, would salute. Then, off we'd go. Before this occurred, Dave ensured we started in the correct, straight positions. At that moment, the horns could dress or straighten out. Then, a ready front command would be given, where the horns would jerk their instruments back in a perpendicular position to be at attention before continuing. Larry ended up with his mouthpiece flying out in the field. However, to prevent the judges from hearing us, we whispered down the line to get Dave's attention so he could return the mouthpiece to Larry (his identical twin). BTW, Larry had a solo during the early part of the show.

After a disappointing show, we were all unhappy as we boarded the bus. A few members expressed their disappointment in no uncertain terms, which only worsened. Eventually, another member started humming Glory, Glory Hallelujah. Then, little by little, more guys joined in. But as the swear words continued to get louder, the humming countered. Eventually, everyone started singing the words, and the tense situation dissipated.

Pieces of Dreams

During another awful performance, the entire bus withdrew into silence. Finally, one brave soul yelled, "Well folks, now for the scores, and we know we have all winners here with us tonight! And now in last place, with a score of zero..."

One day, as the horn line ran some chord exercises, a cute Beagle dog would begin to howl each time they stopped. Oh, how I wish I had a recording of that one.

Eventually, it was off to the World Open finals on August 3rd, 1973, in Lynn, MA. I have looked forward to this competition for a long time. I cannot recall if we went a day or so earlier to rehearse, but this scorching August day was challenging for us all. The instructors asked someone to pick up some food as we continued practicing. During one break, a few people asked what each person wanted, and the situation was getting complicated. Instructor Pepe quickly straightened that out as he yelled, "Just go get a bunch of hamburgers and put ketchup on all of 'em!"

This would be my first experience with a large crowd—thousands. We worked hard all season to make a comeback, and these finals were our best shot at regaining our momentum. We marched as well as we could, hoping to be in the top ten. Now, we awaited the scores. Our realistic goal was to qualify for the final competition. When the preliminary scores finally arrived, we heard our numbers and realized we had been successful. We all jumped around for joy.

The next big contest was the US Open Prelims, and we had a tough time. We placed 22nd in the preliminaries and did not make the finals. It was still a great experience, but no

World Open Class Prelims 1973

01. Bridgemen 84.15
02. Saint Rita's Brassmen 82.90
03. Purple Lancers 81.40
04. Pembroke Imperials 79.00
05. Blue Rock 77.65
06. CMCC Warriors 77.05
07. Magnificent Yankees 76.00
08. Emerald Cadets 75.00 (hurray)
09. The Thing 74.95
10. Cadets of LaSalle 74.95
11. Kewanee Knights 73.45

World Open Class Finals 1973

01. Bridgemen 87.90
02. Saint Rita's Brassmen 86.25
03. Purple Lancers 84.35
04. CMCC Warriors 79.60
05. Pembroke Imperials 78.80
06. Blue Rock 77.60
07. Magnificent Yankees 75.95
08. The Thing 75.80
09. Cadets of LaSalle 75.75
10. Emerald Cadets 73.40

big final show this time. A few things to recall in Ohio, though. First, many of us were in one of the hotel rooms for a break, just hanging out during our relaxing time. At some point, as drummers often do, we started to jam some rhythms with our sticks on anything in the room. No worries; nothing was damaged. Tables, bedsides, lamps, and books. We really had some great beats going. Many of us, especially drummers, jammed as more and more joined. Many were dancing. This was going great.

Jim and I were at the room entrance (looking in) when we noticed that everyone had stopped dancing and jamming except for Jim and me. "Why are you all stopping? Keep it going, man!" Turning, I saw the well-dressed state police officer staring at us. I stopped, but Jim kept jamming with enthusiasm on a nearby lamp. "My goodness gracious, what's going on! Why is everybody stopping?" Jim spouted. That's when I poked him and pointed to the officer. "Please, I have more important things to do today; keep it down and stop banging on the items," the officer pleaded. We apologized.

One of our members decided to prank an older woman who walked by one of our rooms. Looking at her through the large window, he knocked to get her attention and then pressed 'ham' against the window. For those not familiar with that 70s expression, he pressed his butt cheeks against the glass. Oh, man! Fortunately, she laughed, shaking her head.

On our departure, Rick, John, I, and others were packed and waiting by the bus until we were called to board. Then something unexpected occurred, or another moment to be told. We witnessed something you cannot quite make up. A group of kids, young adults, and crazy Emerald Cadets, including a few men, rushed out of the hotel with a bed mattress, trying to fit it through the bus door and into the bus. We stared at this unique event with amazement. All this stuff might not be word-for-word or precisely what happened, but I'm doing my best.

Anyway, Mr M, one of our great, kind, and patient chaperones who happened to be a United States Marine, came running out of the hotel and yelling a few words in a Marine sergeant's voice. The kids quickly brought the mattress back to its proper place. Well, that explanation might have been longer than the final competition explanation. I think my buddies and I were speechless. We certainly had fun and did some really crazy things. Still, I want to emphasize this to everyone: we never damaged any property. We had respect for people and property. We worked hard but had fun. I am in no way suggesting anyone should do some of these things. I don't recommend it.

Speaking of the great United States Marine Corps, "The Commandant's Own" Drum and Bugle Corps was founded in 1934. The parade was so impressive that we wanted a better look at these incredible Marines and musicians. As we neared the snare line, someone said, "That must be so cool to do this in the Marine Corps." Then, one of the Marines laughed and said, "Don't do it! They'll screw ya!" We got a pretty good laugh. Then the commander, thinking he heard something, ran to the area and looked closely at the group. Nope, no one said a word!

Ah, the bus breakdown. The buses were from the 1940s (like the ones in the movie A League of Their Own), but ours were green for the Emerald Cadets. We had two buses and an equipment truck, but the one I rode in broke down and separated from the others. So, we left the bus and were directed to stay away from the highway until the second bus returned. Of course, a few kids had to climb up and sit atop the sign next to the highway. A state police car pulled over, rolled down its window, and yelled, "What the heck are you kids doing on top of a sign on this highway?" "We are waiting for a bus!" "There's no bus coming down here!" Then his radio sounded, and he stated, "I've got an emergency. Get off that dang sign and stay away from the highway!" Shortly after that encounter, another state police car rolled down his window and yelled to the kids on the sign, "Are you the kids waiting for a bus!?" One yelled, "Yep!" Then he said, "Please get off the sign and away from the highway!" It was a long day, but we made it through.

As the 1973 season ended, Emerald would begin preparing for the 1974 season. This coming year would bring many new experiences, and my buddies and I were no longer rookies. Jim was about to head to the newly built Disney World in Florida to play full-time in the Fife and Drum Corps "The Spirit of America." What a fantastic opportunity for him. I was so sad to see him go, but I understood that decision. He was also closer to aging out of junior corps. Many years later, I would have had the opportunity to audition. Still, for various reasons, I decided not to, so it never came to fruition.

One day, after a private lesson, Mr Sturtze turned and looked at my drum set. "Can you play that thing!?" I said,

"Yes, sir!" "Got a minute to play something for me?" I played something from a Buddy Rich album, and he got a real kick. "Not bad," he smiled.

Around this time, I received my last lesson from Mr Sturtze. He wished me luck. I didn't want it to end, but it was that time. We would keep in touch, and I always considered him a great instructor, friend, and part of my family.

Michael H Fiondella Jr

A Successful Failure

As I grew older, I learned more about World War II. Even though my dad and uncles rarely discussed it, their experiences always intrigued me. There are no words for the sacrifices that generation made. I'm not sure any generation could match theirs. Fortunately, my dad's ship never encountered a U-boat torpedo. However, at times, I recall them talking about scary experiences.

But my dad had them laughing when he shared a story about a shipmate on an island. They were on the sidelines watching some sacred marriage ceremony. Dad's shipmate made some noise, and Dad and his shipmate nearly got speared. That's all the details I remember.

I could never burn my draft card, but I wondered about our involvement during the Vietnam War. My uncle William said he always felt something extra for the veterans of the Korean War (the forgotten war) and the Vietnam War. I'll say I always had and will always have the highest regard and respect for all our veterans. If it weren't for them, there's no way we could live with our current freedoms. There's plenty to discuss, but that's not for this book.

It used to annoy me whenever I heard my parents say how quickly time passed. However, I miss them so much and wish I could listen to them now.

Rick and I had a teacher with very eccentric teaching methods. For instance, he'd stand on his desk, pretending to wave flags. "…and the Marseille!" he'd yell. That would send us into hysterics, which unfortunately got us our first and only detention.

Over the intercom, right before dismissal, the announcer said, "The following are to report to room 103 …Michael Fiondella…" My cousin Cathy and others were in shock when they heard my name. As I walked into the room, I didn't notice that Rick was there, but Mr Sylvester and the driver's ed instructor said, "What the heck are you doing here?" "Well," I replied, "I was in class and…" "Get the heck out of here and go home!" Mr Sylvester stated. "Okay, thanks." As I headed out, I heard one fellow ask, "Can I go too?" "Shut up and stay in your seat!" Mr Sylvester yelled. Rick and I got released. Later, arriving home, Dad asked, "What the heck happened?" I explained the scenario, and he said, "Okay, but I do not want to hear that again." Yikes.

Mr Sturtze had urged me to join the high school band. He felt the overall percussion experience would be a good idea, in addition to drum corps and drum set drumming. Although I respected the talent, I was reluctant to adopt that style. It just wasn't something I was interested in. In any event, I did take his advice and joined the band at Sheehan High School in my senior year. It would be a rewarding experience, especially in the concert band, where I learned more and performed on various percussion instruments.

At Sheehan High School, preparations were made for the production of the play Funny Girl. The orchestra pit required a percussionist, and our music director, Mr Houlahan, asked if I was interested. However, I was reluctant because I had never missed a drum and bugle corps competition. But his insistence was a compliment. I was concerned when I approached the Emerald Cadets instructing staff. They were disappointed, but they understood that it was an educational commitment.

At one Sheehan Band practice, Mr Houlahan stopped the entire band and looked up at me. "Mr Fiondella, we do not roll like that here." "How would you like the roll?" I asked. "More pressed together." So, I did, and Rick got a real kick out of that.

There were several rehearsals for the play. I recall one or two professional musicians from New York who assisted with the Funny Girl scores.

It turned out to be a rewarding experience. Getting assistance and praise from other professional musicians and the audience was terrific. However, it was the only time Rick and I missed a drum corps show.

Dad and Mom supported my interest in music. Mom, being a great musician, understood this better than anyone. Dad was concerned about my future and encouraged me to continue my education.

I desired to obtain training in self-defense. Joe, a family friend, introduced me to a martial arts school in East

Haven, Connecticut, run by Sensei Joe P. Joe was also a New Haven police officer and served as an instructor. I added this to my schedule and attended classes throughout the winter months when the drum corps wasn't competing as much. After I committed to this school, my cousin Rich, a great martial artist, began teaching at his new school. By the way, his sister (my cousin Lynn) was another wonderful person to see and talk to.

I admired martial artists Bruce Lee and Chuck Norris, as well as boxers Rocky Marciano and Muhammad Ali. I thought it was cool how Ali would put his hands down and fight, yet his opponents would still miss. Of course, I had to try this in martial arts class. However, after a few hits, including a busted nose, I finally learned what NOT to do. Sensei Joe taught a variety of arts, blending them together with an emphasis on the practical aspects. His focus was Shotokan (meaning empty hand in Okinawa, Japan).

"Did you ever spar with your instructor?" some would ask. "Sure, and I beat the crap out of him." "What do you mean?" Then I'd say, "Well, I beat the crap out of his hands with my face." In one class, I ended up with a black eye. Of course, when I got home, Mom reacted. "Oh my, what happened? Get one of Dad's steaks and place it on your eye." Then Dad reacted, "Don't use one of my five-dollar Delmonicos; get some ice." I got some ice.

That reminds me of when my brother Bill bumped into Muhammad Ali at an airport. A few big guards hurried to stop him as he walked towards him. "What are you doing? "I would like to get his autograph, if possible," Bill stated.

Pieces of Dreams

"Let him pass, it's okay," Ali replied graciously. "So, who's your favorite fighter?" "Joe Frazier!" my jokester brother announced. Ali grabbed my brother's paper and signed it. Bill never forgot how personable Ali was.

I attended a Grand Funk Railroad concert with Joe and Mary at the New Haven Colosseum. I remember looking down from our above-center seats while they played "We're an American Band." It was a good concert.

The Emerald Cadets fared well in Connecticut in 1974. Great friends, great fun, and great memories. So much more was yet to come.

One of my nephews was playing at a local football game in North Brandford. My brother asked if Rick and I could play the National Anthem. We were glad to do it, but we didn't want to mess that up. As Rick and I walked onto the field, he asked, "Are you nervous about this?" I said, "Nah, I'm just rolling on this one; you've got the melody." He shook his head. We played well.

I have never tried drugs. I might have had a beer now and then, but the drug scene irritated me. I wish people would think harder before getting involved.

I mention this because one of my good friends almost died. I had no idea he got into something heavy. Fortunately, all ended well. I remember him later confessing, "Your true friends won't encourage you to take any of this stuff and will dissuade you from doing so." It disgusts me to think how much money people make from selling drugs. When we had parties, no one pressured each other. I am not trying to sound politically correct. Still, we always had a designated driver, even though it wasn't emphasized as much as it is today. Luckily, we just had common sense.

On one occasion, some of my buddies and I decided to go to Riverside Amusement Park in Agawam, Mass, which is now called Six Flags New England. Back then (ages ago), the loop and metal roller coasters were relatively new. Louie was in a seat behind me (a great horn player who was usually quiet and reserved but funny as heck, who would mutter things under his breath). So, off we went for the loop, but the dang thing got stuck at the top. Fortunately, we weren't wholly upside-down, but now what? While waiting for help, a younger kid was shaken up, but we were able to calm him down. But Louie started goofing off, screaming, "We're all gonna die! This is it! We're all gonna die!" Oh man, that got the kid going all over again. But then, just as quickly, Louie sat there like nothing had happened. Gradually, we were pushed, and everything returned to normal. I wonder if that kid experienced recurring nightmares.

At this point in my life, I spent much of my time thinking about a potential career. My passion for music was at least equal to that of anyone else who had music on their mind. Looking back on it now, I can't fully express just how deep this passion was, except for a few close friends. This passion would cause me to bounce around from college to college and several schools until I finally found a straighter path. With that said, high school became another memory.

What was I to do? I received many pamphlets in the mail from various colleges and universities. I investigated a few of them, but was unsure.

Pieces of Dreams

Rick and I decided to visit the Citadel Military College of South Carolina. So, we boarded a jetliner (my first), and I reflected on Uncle William's wartime experience. As the jet approached the runway, we came to a stop. Then, we saw the pilot (or co-pilot) walk to the back of the plane. I said, "Shouldn't he be in the cockpit?" "I think so!" Rick chided. But we never discovered the reason for his stroll down the aisle.

As we checked out the school, we found it incredible. Discipline, honor, and respect were the foundations of everything. "Don't do it!" a passerby joked. "They'll screw ya!" However, I was mesmerized by everything I witnessed, and the military-style band was a particularly captivating attraction. I wasn't ready for college and didn't know which path to take. Still, thanks to my family and others, I was so grateful to have the opportunity to decide my future. My parents said they would pay for at least one semester if I wanted to enter military school. It was a fortunate situation. I know it took a lot for my parents to save that money. So, it was to be. I decided to try it and entered the school of civil engineering.

Arriving in August was interesting, to say the least. It reminded me of the time I was five, requesting a Beatles haircut but getting a butch instead. I really don't consider myself to be cocky, but I had a lot of confidence and liked to laugh and kid around because life is just too short. As the officer stood next to me, I told the barber, "Just take a little of the sides." The officer responded, "We have a live one here." I should have known then, as I do now, that sometimes it's not good to attract attention. They provided us with the same clothes and materials, along with plenty of instructions. I learned how to eat square meals, i.e., small portions, by going straight up with the fork, then at a ninety-degree angle to your mouth, and back down the same way. I learned to say, Sir, before and after each sentence.

Freshmen received special treatment, whether they wanted it or not. I love ketchup, especially hamburgers, so I asked. "Sir, cadet recruit Fiondella requests permission to put ketchup on his hamburger, sir!" He answered, "What do you think this is, you idiot, a resort?"

I must have set the record for laughing push-ups. "Sir, ha ha hee hee ho ho, Sir, Sir one Sir! Sir, ha ha hee hee ho ho, Sir, Sir two Sir." Ya, that was me. Officer Rivera would let me have it, yet we both laughed. "Fiondella, I don't know what it is with you, but I will have to get someone else to let you have it because I cannot do it!" Believe me, he did send a special guest upperclassman to 'let me have it,' and I got it alright.

There was another tough upperclassman, but I made an unofficial bet that I could get rid of him. "Sir! I thought I heard that you have a phone call, Sir!" He left to inquire, and much to my amazement, nothing happened. I thought it was good luck. Later that day, I was inundated by several upperclassmen and quickly discovered that no one got away with anything. I think I broke the push-up world record until I could no longer lift myself from the ground. I learned a lesson that day.

Being that music was still very much a part of me, I, of course, wanted and needed to audition for a band company. Several others were in the room when it was my turn to audition. "You can relax here; we want to ascertain your level to see if you'd be a good fit," the cadet at the desk said. We read music and play a variety of songs. The marching band plays an important role. And we probably use a little more rudiments than most other bands." Oh, this sounded fantastic! I thought I did well at sight-reading, but I knew I had some practice ahead.

As a reminder, the single-stroke roll (L-R-L-R-L-R) should be equally separated smooth beats. Flams (LR-RL-LR-RL): the first tap in each spot here are grace notes, which are more lightly played, usually two inches or lower. The second beat is higher and louder, and it should produce a distinctive clicking sound when played. The long roll (LLRRLLRRLLRR) should be equally separated smooth beats, with bouncing separated smooth beats when fast. Single paradiddle (LRLLRLRR), evenly spaced beats with the first and 5th beat accented and the remaining taps at about six inches. One more example is the single ratamacue LL-R-L-R-L, which involves rest and opposite sticking.

"Okay, we would like to see some rudiments. Do you know what they are?" "Yes, sir." As he asked me to play a few of the basic rudiments, I played each well. "You seem pretty knowledgeable, so let's try something trickier. Let's see your single ratamacue!" Again, I played it without a hitch. After I finished, there was a group discussion. "Okay, pretty good; we'll see you soon." I made it!

I became great friends with Steve, and we tried to keep in touch and keep each other sane. I got along with everyone, and many newbies would confide in me. A few of the guys gave me the nickname Priest. Several freshmen I knew left school within a few weeks, including the guy I flew down with from Chester, Connecticut. Many newbies wound up leaving—military school was not for them. I decided to stick it out for the time being, but I spent a lot of time contemplating my future.

They filmed the Columbo episode, By Dawn's Early Light, at the Citadel, and I ended up as an extra. You can't see me because I was just one of the many freshmen running around in some of the scenes. That was a blast. When Columbo was in the phone booth, I stood only a few feet away, waiting for our next scene.

I also remember attending a football game and marching in with the cadets. Wow! There were some strange moments, too. When we finally got to walk to town, Steve and I decided to get an ice cream. However, we were advised not to walk alone in some areas. How sad. I remember walking through a neighborhood with Steve when I was a kid, about seven or eight. He was running down his driveway with a garbage can top, winging it at us and just missing our heads. The mother never said a thing.

My roommate and I got along well, but we had different interests.

The college would have occasional dances (inviting a local girls' school). I remember meeting a pleasant young lady who asked some of us to dinner at her house. The family was so gracious. Her father would sneak brownies in for me when he delivered the laundry. I would hide them as best as I could. But I'm sure the officers or upperclassmen knew about all of it.

Pieces of Dreams

I was at attention with my snare drum outside before we played around the campus. Then, upperclassmen in the band stopped and asked, "So you think you're a pretty good drum player?" I said, "Sir, yes, sir!" "Do you think you're better than me!?" I said, "Sir, yes, sir!" After a short discussion with a friend, he said, "Play something!" So, I did. "Play something again!" So, I did, but it was more complicated. "We might talk with you about a quartet, but we usually don't talk to you knobs, so best watch your step." "Sir, yes, sir."

I knew I would not continue at the Citadel. I was homesick, but not enough to drive me to make rash decisions. During my brief time there, I learned many valuable lessons about the college and the ROTC program. I even took martial arts for a time.

There were strict rules everywhere, even at the mess hall. Upperclassmen would sit at the ends of the table, and our knobs would sit at the sides. If an upperclassman raised his glass, the person or knob next to him was supposed to instantly take his glass and fill it with water from the container on the table. Some things were really 'out there,' but that's part of the whole point—taking the pressure.

Another freshman next to me seemed highly nervous during one particular eating fest. He appeared to be in a panic. The uneasy freshman didn't see the upperclassman raise his glass. Uh-oh! Suddenly, the upperclassmen let go of the glass, but luckily, I caught it, filled it with water, and placed it in front of him. I got a look, but all remained calm. This poor kid was shaking. I didn't see him after that, but I hoped he was okay. I wasn't about to stay for several reasons, but fear wouldn't be my downfall.

Since my parents paid for that first semester, I could decide if I wanted to continue. Thinking back, I should have thought about everything in more detail. Live and learn. It certainly was an honor to be in a military environment. Still, I ended up staying for only two or three more months. I need a new direction, but looking back, I had it much easier than most new cadets. If I recall correctly, they gave preferential treatment to band members. I had first-floor privileges, whereas most new cadets had to use the stairs, asking for permission each time.

Every morning, reveille would be played, and everyone on campus would stop and salute the flag. That was just a cool, unique thing. Once, as I was running back to my room, I noticed the bugler held in contention (or maybe he was ordered to stay in his room). I took a chance, stopped, and asked, "What the heck are you doing in there?" he responded with his southern accent, "I was playing reveille this morning, and I cracked." I couldn't help but laugh. I was in the Navy ROTC. I remember the first ROTC class where we all sat quietly, waiting for this strong Marine to start class. He had all kinds of stripes on his shirt. Suddenly, he smacked the desk hard with his hand; some jumped as he rose. "How many of you here are Marines ROTC!?" Some raised their hands. How many are in the Navy ROTC?" Some raised their hands. He shouted, "Who's the first to hit the beaches, the Marines!" All I could think of then and now is that I'm glad he was on our side.

I'll never forget when an upperclassman came into my room and said, "So early on, we actually had you in mind to be a squad leader next year." He gave me one of his corporal stripes and wished me luck. One of my last discussions was with a major from the Air Force, who had a lengthy conversation about my decision to remain at the school. He also discussed this with my dad. However, my father wanted me to make my own decision. By the way, I believe my dad trained new Navy recruits at one point when he was in the Navy. It was a difficult decision, but I decided to leave. It was terrible that I waited months, so no refund was given to my parents. I went and left with an honorable discharge on good terms. It was a short experience, and I will never forget it.

I suppose it's the respect I always had for all in the military, even though the 1960s and 1970s were trying times. I was proud of my family's military history. Nonetheless, I knew it was time to make some critical decisions, and I was fortunate and blessed not to be drafted. Fortunately, or unfortunately, that would take a little more time for me. Still, I considered this to be a successful failure.

Michael H Fiondella Jr

1974

I returned home. Dad knew right away that music was still engraved in me and that I had considered music school all along. Mom was Mom, and she would support me no matter what. The hesitation was undoubtedly there. First, most music students' primary instrument is usually not percussion. I knew some piano, but I didn't know enough at the college level. It was frustrating. Like many college students who change their majors, I was no exception, as I was making changes too.

Emerald Cadets started preparing for the next season, and many girls ran up to me on my first time back and rubbed my shaved head. Many new members would join, including a snare drummer named Al, who would become another great friend. Emerald Cadets' repertoire for this season would be American Patrol, Variations on America, In the Mood, Boogie Woogie Bugle Boy, Madam Butterfly, and If I Ruled the World. We were all optimistic and looking forward to a good year. I was so happy to be back in Drum Corps again. This affected me likely more than family and friends ever knew. I just wanted to perform in some fashion. For now, it was back to drum corps music, and I was certainly thinking of a future career.

Michael H Fiondella Jr

I was aware of several snare drum competitions that interested me. It was challenging for unpaid performers, especially young performers, to gather from coast to coast. However, I heard about the Connecticut Hurricanes Drum and Bugle Corps sponsoring an open individual competition, including a snare event. Unfortunately, I do not believe anyone from the West Coast participated.

I practiced and practiced and practiced. Many may not realize how physical this could become. A typical individual rehearsal might include several warmups such as single right beats, then single left beats, then accented within single beats, then triplet sevens, RLRLRLR – L, and repeat, LRLRLRL - R and repeat, then nines, RLRLRLRLR – L. Then I would exercise rolls, let's say at 120 or 130 beats per minute or RRLLRRLLRR. At one point, I did include a long roll or RRLLRRLLRRLL that continued for forty-five minutes straight. Once, my wrists actually became totally numb, and the sticks just fell out of my hands.

That competition finally arrived. Unfortunately, Mom, Dad, and Grandma were unable to attend. Family and friends wished me luck. John offered to drive me so I could concentrate on the competition.

The building was very crowded. This would be my first time playing in front of a large crowd alone. Yes, I was nervous, but I learned to control it. Mr Sturtze and John Bodnar were my backbone.

I remember the moment I approached the judge. Not easy at all. The first thing I thought of was Pop. The judge allowed me to do a brief warmup. Then I saluted, and he returned the salute; it was the moment of truth. I attacked

Pieces of Dreams

this snare solo like never before. This moment and preparation for this competition might never happen again. I felt confident and drummed my butt off. My arms and wrists were moving more accurately and faster than ever before. The room was filled with several hundred people. When I finished, there was a loud roar! What a great feeling! My very first big snare drumming individuals.

I used to pride myself on fast, clean, flam phrasings (for non-drummers, these parts would have distinctive click sounds for one tap or beat). If missed, this could create a substantial popping sound noticeable to non-players.

Now, I waited for the scores. I waited and waited and waited. Later that evening, the scores were finally announced. In 3rd place... in 2nd place... in first place, my name! I was numb. So grateful. Mr Sturtze would place me on his student champion list for The Hurricanes Open Nationals. An article featuring this and part of Mr Sturtze's student champions would later be presented in the Northeast Drum Corps News in June 1977. I arrived home with tons of congratulations. I will always treasure this memory. Dad joked, saying, "Maybe that and ten cents would get you a cup of coffee." I laughed. No matter how old I was, Mom was Mom. "Congratulations, that's so nice. Would you like some cookies and milk?" My eyebrows went up!

More time would pass...

I heard Mom yelling for Dad, but my father didn't answer. We could finally move the door enough to get in. He must have fainted against the door. He was conscious but not in a good state. We tried calling my aunt Millie, but as luck would have it, her phone was busy (remember, only landlines existed at the time). So, Mom dialed emergency while I ran to Aunt Millie's house in my socks in the snow. While she was getting the keys to her car, I ran back in my socks in the snow. She arrived and assisted, and the ambulance took Dad to Meriden Hospital.

What an experience. It was a scary moment. I drove there. However, no parking was available, so I pulled into an out-of-the-way area. Diagnosis—a severe ulcer, but thankfully, all would be okay. On a lighter note, I ended up with a parking ticket. Later, I told Dad, "This is nuts. It was an emergency. I'll explain my case to the police. I'm sure they'll let it go." Dad responded, "No way, you'll pay the ticket, and I'll take ya!" Eyebrows up again!

Holy Moly, Huh! Yep, I paid the ticket.

Back to drum corps... I believe one of the most significant innovations ever was the introduction of the tuned bass drum section. According to my research, the Chicago Cavaliers were among the first to utilize tuned-pitched bass drums. Additionally, Gerry Shellmer and the Boston Crusaders conceived numerous innovative ideas in the 1960s and 1970s, particularly with the entire drum section. Gerry's influence included marching tympani, keyboards, ride cymbals, concert bass drums, and cymbals. His drum parts were absolutely astonishing. I haven't heard better-syncopated parts from anyone else. Think of several bass drum players, each having different pitches, acting like a single bass guitar player within a band. Incredible coordination.

Pieces of Dreams

Some of his genius included extraordinarily rhythmical drum solos. As one listened, they made people want to dance. Some percussion solos included a jazz version of Pop Goes The Weasel and Dave Brubeck's Unsquare Dance. Think of the challenge of playing physically demanding parts accurately and cleanly while attempting to march in 7/4 time. Look up the Boston Crusaders of the late 1960s and early 1970s to see what I mean. There will be more on him later.

Rick and Gregg had a duo in Boogie Woogie Bugle Boy, and I had a small drum break in a makeshift drum set where fellow and great drummer Dee Dee placed her triple drums next to me. Dee was a great drummer, carrying those heavy triples at a time when there were not many girls in drum lines. Lynn played snare and was great at it. Lynn's sister, Gail, was a tremendous soprano bugle player. I never had an issue with women being in the corps. I respected everyone's talents.

One very hot summer day, after surviving a long parade, many of us, including Rick, John, Louie, Dave, Al, and me, decided to get something nice and cold. Ice cream, anyone?! As Al couldn't wait to dip into that first scoop, a fly decided to dive bomb straight into his dish. His usual Ahhhhhnmm, his bummed out sound rang out! Back in line, Al.

Al had some unique sounds. After one of our very late nights after a show and party, and with little sleep to get up quite early for a parade. Because of our crazy schedule, he slept at my house. Al released a refreshing "ah" when the alarm went off with the great Olivia Newton-John singing, Have You Never Been Mellow.

One popular drum solo was Crazy Army. It was a more syncopated rhythm that gained popularity later. Emerald had a pretty cool street beat with a crazy army-type rhythm, a long, extended roll at the end, and a cool triple toms beat.

It was a nice feeling performing at so many events. We would win and lose some, but we always had a great time. It was rewarding to hear the crowd cheer us on, even if it was sometimes deafening.

Another very memorable moment was a competition with the Hawthorne Muchachos. They were at a higher level than us and one of the country's top junior corps in the United States (arguably, the U.S. had the best drum and bugle corps in the world). They were well-respected, and their talent blew us away. We loved their Latin-style show.

It might have been one of our snare lines' best performances. We came within a fraction of the Muchachos drum score, which would only happen in this show. I wish I could explain the vantage point from our perspective. I wish I had a recording of that show. The power behind the show is difficult to put into words. It's so cool. Snares, toms or triples, bass drums, tympani, cymbals, and the added marimbas. Other corps on the Muchachos level included the unique and traditional Garfield Cadets, the Bayonne Bridgemen, and the 27th Lancers. Please listen to some of them when you can, both new and old recordings.

Pieces of Dreams

I had a terrific day in New Jersey when anyone from anywhere could compete against each other in an individual competition. It was a blessing and a curse because I believe (perhaps a little biased) that I would have received a higher rating if the judges had relied strictly on technicality. However, modern contests began focusing on entertainment, such as stick twirling, which isn't always a bad thing. Nevertheless, I've always felt that the technical side should take precedence. Still, as time passed, entertainment began to be valued more.

I could have added more showmanship while maintaining the technical aspects. But no excuses, no biggie. During the competition, I was warming up with some problematic flam phrases. In any case, I played this type of beat within a more complicated phrase, where providing a distinctive click would be very difficult. Once, a younger competitor noticed and asked, "What the heck are you playing?" "I was attempting to play flams within some difficult areas." He loved it and was very complimentary. I'm always grateful and appreciative when other drummers take notice. Anyhow, I was able to capture first place.

Between competitions, Al and I decided to work on a snare drumming duet, including a challenging solo. We wanted to present an entertaining solo but still focus on complex snare parts. It was enjoyable. One section of the solo had some fast one-handed singles on the left hand. During most of the solo, we needed to perform as one, ensuring exact stick heights and precise arm and motion positioning. During the last left-handed singles, we witnessed one judge's pipe fall out of his mouth while we did our best to keep our composure. Yup, we aced it and came in first. Of course, this didn't always happen, but it's nice to emphasize the times we did! :-)

The Drum Corps International (DCI) was gaining popularity. These drum and bugle corps were becoming the best in the world. In 2005, a video titled DCI Athletes was released. It's worth watching on YouTube.

We would venture to see other drum corps shows, including the DCI shows. I'll say Wow! Given my situation, I thought it unlikely I would ever have the chance to march in a DCI show. I hoped that, somehow, the Emerald Cadets could build to that level. We knew it was unlikely in our situation. We were a strong corps, but we needed financial backing and other resources. Some of us discussed the possibility of a type of super corps existing. Then, it began happening with the DCI during the summer months. Our thoughts were becoming a reality.

Many of my buddies and I returned from a show exhausted, so we pulled into a truck stop to rest. The next thing I knew, I woke up on the sidewalk with my feet up on the car bumper and the sound of a lawnmower approaching. Al was asleep on the car roof while the others snoozed inside. Oh, man!

Another time, Rick was driving, and I was in the passenger seat as we approached a toll booth. "Could you grab some change? I'm out," Rick intoned. "Do you mean out completely, no cash, no change, no nothing?" "Yep!" I looked everywhere. "Well, that makes two of us, we're out!" Not a cent to be had between the two of us. "We got nothin'! Now what?" I whined. Now, at the booth, Rick rolled down his window, removed his glasses, and moaned, "I—just—don't—have—it!" The tool booth attendant gave us a pathetic look, "Oh, go ahead!" Whew!

As the bus was getting ready to depart, we noticed a crew from Channel 8 from New Haven, Connecticut, so John decided to play the entire Ch 8 theme out the window with his soprano bugle.

At one point, I was given the unofficial title of Drum Sergeant, responsible for leading the drum section. I was proud and honored. I was usually passive and patient when learning new things. However, on one occasion, I was exasperated when members kept turning at the wrong time. "Please concentrate. This should not be happening after all this time." So, during the show, you guessed it, I was the one who turned when I wasn't supposed to. Nothing like facing thousands of people by yourself. I made believe I had a solo and hurried back in line. Yes, you guessed it. They never let me forget it. By the way, while confessing, I only dropped the stick once in all the shows I played.

Michael H Fiondella Jr

Is It Done?

A very different year was about to unfold. As usual, we began practice in the fall, but now we were very experienced. Meanwhile, Dad continued to work hard, and Mom treated everyone like family. Grandma, of course, was her usual angelic self. My buddies and I would often venture out on weekends to see movies, attend parties, and the like. All in good taste. Rick was now in college, and John was at a technical school. Ultimately, I arrived at a decision that made sense. Thanks to having a little time to decide, my family, Gregg, my first great Electronics boss and neighbor, and I decided to attend The Connecticut School of Electronics. This would give me a fascinating field and career ahead. Of course, this means no chance of joining the DCI Corps. This would become a twenty-four-month continuous training course. A decision had to be made.

I realized how fortunate I was in my situation. At the same time, I would continue playing my drum set in my basement apartment, listening to all types of rock and jazz, and practicing rudimental drumming for many hours to perfect that style. One of my best friends, Dave, who was out on his own at sixteen with a job and an apartment, told me to enjoy a few years with my family while I could, as it would make it easier to acquire an education. Thinking about that now gives me the chills. Imagine getting such priceless advice from a sixteen-year-old. Dave P was a dedicated and hardworking individual, as well as an excellent horn player. Many prominent individuals from companies, organizations, and politics might benefit from heeding common sense, as he did.

I'm so lucky again to have the family and friends I have. My nephew needed to have specific surgery on the hip area (if memory serves me correctly). This ended well, but it would take a considerable time to heal. When we visited him at the children's hospital, I remember seeing many children who needed help. With only modest donations, I wished we could do so much more. I felt very uncomfortable and realized that the medical field may never be for me. I could not take seeing people, especially kids, in pain. I went into a rest area, sat down, and rested my head, holding my hands to my face. Breath! A nurse stopped. "Sir, are you alright?" Imagine that. "Ya, but I don't understand how you can work here." Sitting beside me, she said, "You cannot look at it like that. Or overthink it. We are here to help." Interesting take.

Christmas 1974. My Mom prepared a fantastic dinner for Dad, Grandma, Bill, my nephew, and me. The snow was coming down hard, so Bill rigged up a clever contraption that was safe for Drew to transport, who needed a wheelchair for a while. He was healing and in a talkative mood. My brother (normally quiet and laid back) began joking with Drew. "Please, quiet down for a minute. I'm getting a headache." But Drew kept excitedly yapping. Hey, it was Christmas, after all. Bill calmly repeated what he had said to him earlier as we ate. Still, Drew carried on. Brother Bill repeated. Drew kept excitedly yapping. Brother Bill repeated. Drew continued. Finally, Bill got up, grabbed the wheelchair, opened the sliding door, placed Drew on the deck in the snowstorm, and closed the door. My Mom panicked (a rare occurrence). She yelled at Bill, but Drew thought it funny and laughed hysterically.

I'm forever grateful to Gregg Cocco for facilitating my love for music and interest in electronics. Due to his inspiration, I could walk many paths and pursue an electronics diploma (a twenty-four-month course), thus becoming an electronics technician (later, I would pursue a degree in electrical engineering). Naturally, this hindered travel or joining any highly rated DCI corps. It was a huge bummer for me, and no one else realized how much of a toll it had taken. But it wouldn't last forever, and I had to repeatedly remind myself.

I worked on and off at the Oakdale Musical Theatre, where I had the opportunity to witness many great musicians. A drummer I spoke with mentioned that he loved what he did, but living out of a suitcase was not all fun and games. Music would continue to be my passion, but I had to take a different path.

I was lucky enough to be living at home. My parents were old-fashioned, and we certainly had a traditional family structure. I recall people asking if Italians were constantly at odds with each other because they tended to yell a lot. They showed an exuberance for life. It was 'love yelling,' I explained.

One evening, while taking a study break, I went upstairs to sit with my grandmother. She was flicking through channels, looking for something to watch. Grandma said she was exhausted, and her hands were sore, so she needed a break from knitting. She ended up watching a football game, which was unusual for her. "Michael, I'm curious; I've been watching this game for a while and trying to understand it. These men on one team seem to be trying to get the ball to one side of the field, but they're hurting each other awfully. Then, the other team seems to be trying to get the ball to the other side of the field and doing the same. I don't understand this game!" "Ah, I think you understand this game better than anyone else," I replied.

During an extensive snowstorm, the roads were impassable, so Dad walked down the street to a local store. I watched TV near the sliding glass door with Mom and Grandma. Looking through it, I saw Dad walking up the hill with a bag of groceries. Then, due to a snowbank, we momentarily lost sight of him. But all we could see were apples and oranges rolling down the hill, quickly followed by my father running downhill. By the time he entered the house, we were all in hysterics. Poor Dad. No explanation is needed.

It was time for another snare drum contest at the Hurricanes Nationals. During a long rehearsal in my basement apartment, I struggled with a section of a solo. After numerous tries and not connecting, I took an uncharacteristic action. I threw one of my drumsticks across the room, baseball style. But instead of bouncing, the stick was firmly stuck in the wall. Then I heard a thud, followed by Dad opening the door. "What was that? Are you okay?" "Ya, I dropped my stick," I lied. Oh boy.

From then on, a Raquel Welch poster covered my fit of anger. I'm not proud of that moment. Eventually, I nailed the part without any more outbursts. I won the National Open Snare Championship two years in a row. I squeaked by a drummer named Steve, who was a few years younger. This kid was quite the drummer at age fifteen. We were always competing with each other, taking turns winning, but we remained good friends.

Al was next to me in the snare line, performing rim-accented flams. But when we were supposed to remain silent, Al let out an extended "ugh"! It was then that our synchronization went to la la land. After we had left the field, I said, "I heard a weird sound. What happened?" He then showed me his hand. He caught his finger between the rim and the stick during the accented part and cut himself. Think of one big hammer with the edge striking your finger. Poor Al. Ouch.

Some of us would still travel to see the newly formed DCI's incredible performances (there are so many great examples to choose from, with just a very few examples that follow, so please forgive me if I left anyone out that you like).

- Muchachos: first number in 1975 with Jeff Kievit's solo

- Santa Clara's: drum line parts and solos, the fugue part, "Bring in the Clowns", the bottle dance, and the 1975 show. In 2008, Ballet for Martha.

- Garfield Cadets: all their shows, especially their traditional corps song, "Oh, Holy Name." In later years (1983-1985), they became the first DCI corps to earn three consecutive DCI titles. And in 1987, Appalachian Spring.

- Madison Scouts: "MacArthur Park" and "The Way We Were"

- Cavaliers: "Somewhere Over the Rainbow"

- The 27th Lancers: "Danny Boy"

- Bridgemen: "A Few of My Favorite Things" and "Land of Make Believe"

- Blue Devils: "Legend of the One-Eyed Sailor" and "Channel One Suite"

- Boston Crusaders: All of Gerry Shellmer's drum parts in the 1960s and 1970s

- Anaheim Kingsman: 1972 and first DCI Champions

I competed in the DCI Snare Individuals contest for the first time. I placed 9th out of sixteen. I was highly disappointed. I sure was handed my head on this one. No excuses, but I was stubborn and kept attempting rudimental snare drumming with less flipping of the sticks. Despite the challenge, I liked keeping complex flam phrasing in my solos. Again, no excuses. Looking back on it now, I could have wowed the crowd with more theatrics, but it was what it was. Besides, the sun was in my eyes.

Pieces of Dreams

"If I Ruled the World" was one of the last warm and fuzzy memories of the Emerald Cadets. In 1975, the Emerald Cadets placed 25th out of 46 in the DCI Open Class World championships. When the season ended, Father Mitchell announced that the Emerald Cadets were to disband due to circumstances. For us, it was crushing. I thought about it and figured it was probably my time to call it quits. Some asked, "When will you grow up, get a full-time job, and stop this nonsense?"

Soon, I heard about the Emerald Cadets from New Haven merging with the Golden Buccaneers from Bridgeport, Connecticut. A significant merger and a considerable challenge. The corps would be named the Emerald Buccaneers. Later, my good friends in the corps kept asking me to join. As time passed, I missed it because I'd be out of drum corps for the first time in six years. I was also asked about getting a 3-peat at the Hurricanes Nationals Snare Drum Individuals. Yet, after being out of action for several months, I declined.

After the Emerald Cadets broke up, many changes took place. I heard that snare drummer Lynn and her sister, Gail, the soprano bugle player, decided to travel to the Garfield Cadets in New Jersey, venturing into the DCI Corps. I was happy for them.

Time sure passed quickly... Rick continued with college while John remained at technical school. Dave was working hard at his job.

As always, I attempted to be different. This Halloween, I borrowed my dad's red Eldorado. I drove through the center of good ol' Wallingford, Connecticut, wearing a green pin-striped suit like the Jerry Lewis one. It was an enjoyable night, and I received a few laughs—mission accomplished.

I was finally at the point of having a reasonable reputation as a snare drummer, but now I was a little out of shape. However, I enjoyed playing with local bands when they needed someone to sit in. After several attempts from my corps buddies, I finally visited the newly formed Emerald Buccaneers Drum and Bugle Corps. I recall being wowed to see a nine-person snare drum line, one of the largest around. Quite a challenge keeping nine people together. The horn line was compelling. Eventually (you guessed it), they convinced me to join. I only had a short time left since I'd be twenty-one in a year. It was the bicentennial year, so there would be plenty of demands for our corps.

Due to the merger, we had a unique sound. I wish I could remember everyone's names, but I'll never forget the experience. We were one of the better junior corps in Connecticut.

We were returning to our bus when a few Blue Devils stuck their heads out the windows. "You have ten snares!" "Thanks, but I don't think we'll beat you this year." They arguably had the best drum line in the world, as did the Santa Clara Vanguards. I remember talking with drum corps members from the top DCI corps. They began rehearsing all day, all summer long. They were testing physical and musical limitations. This is why I believe these top junior corps were becoming the best in the world.

Janet was a wonderful person and snare drummer, and she inquired if I could help her with her individual snare solo. I wrote part of the arrangement that began with a typical, simple drum corps rhythm, then segued into a surprisingly tricky section to throw the judges off and surprise everyone. As the scores were announced, she beat me (but no worries, I came back like a tiger in later competitions). "I'm sorry, Mike," she said apologetically. That's okay, I smirked. "I will never help you again!"

Somewhere along the way, I contacted a snare drummer in the Santa Clara Vanguard. His name was Al, just like one of my best friends. He became a good buddy, and we had interesting conversations. I was certainly curious how they obtained their precision and excellence.

Did I have memorable moments in Emerald Buccaneers besides the shows? Certainly.

We were heading to a show on our buses, but stopped somewhere in Bridgeport, Connecticut. Suddenly, a crazy teenager shouts, "Riot time!" That's when all hell broke loose with yelling, screaming, and everyone jumping on one another. Oh man, it was insane. Then Tiny, a gentle giant of a bass drummer, says, "Come on, guys, stop it. Cut it out," he laughed, pushing people far away very easily. Fortunately, the staff calmed us down before things got out of hand.

The Emerald Buccaneers did well, especially for the first year, but did not compete in the highest open class at DCI. Instead, they competed in the DCI Class A division, placing 3rd out of sixteen. The Blue Devils won the open-class championships that year.

Michael H Fiondella Jr

A unique occurrence took place during the 1976 DCI individual snare competition. A friend and Emerald Buccaneer member came running over as I prepared to play my solo. "I overheard kids laughing and making fun of your uniform and corps." That really got me going and inspired me to play even better. I wound up in fifth place. I was proud but frustrated. The guys who beat me were in the top five corps and went on to the finals. Nonetheless, I was still a proud Sturtze student representing my corps. This season came to an end. I never made it to the finals, but the memories were superb. Sadly, the Emerald Buccaneers would disband.

By the way, I saw the DCI Nationals in 1976 in Philadelphia, PA. No words.

Al, from the Santa Clara Vanguard, offered me great advice to try out for their snare line in my last year as a twenty-one-year-old. This was a tough decision because I was about to complete electronics school in the fall and had no job, despite having offers to live with roommates in an apartment. Still, I was concerned about finding work in Santa Clara and owing back rent. I did not want to take advantage of the guys. Additionally, I had to complete the twenty-four-month continuing course at electronics school. I could not expect to travel anytime soon.

I was doing very well and had excellent instructors. Our class was the last to receive a full course of instruction regarding television vacuum tubes. Instruction also included semiconductors and circuit chips at that time.

Pieces of Dreams

Television instruction was all-encompassing because it encompassed audio, video, and radio, and even back then, computer logic was involved. There was so much to learn.

One of my classmates was quite sick at the time. He ended up okay, but missed a few weeks of school. During his absence, we built an AM radio. When he returned, he tried his best to catch up, but he rushed. He was sitting next to me when he plugged it in. Boom! Fiz! Smoke! The whole class jumped up. He calmly unplugged the radio, grabbed his books, and then violently smashed the radio into several pieces.

Mom, Dad, Grandma, and I were watching a Maxwell House coffee commercial. "I rarely say anything bad about someone, so this is very strange, but I dislike this lady for some reason. So why do I dislike this lady so much?" My Mom responded, "Oh my goodness, don't you know who that is? She played the Wicked Witch in The Wizard of Oz. You were so deathly afraid of her that you couldn't finish the movie." Now that's different. Yikes.

I decided to spend time attempting to figure out the Santa Clara Vanguard's first number, Entrance of the Emperor and His Court. It was quite a challenge. After finally figuring out the snare drum parts (from an album), I set up my borrowed MacIntosh audio system to record myself with their drum line. Adjusting and re-adjusting the electronics system, including the mics, amps, and drums, took considerable time. I wanted to blend my snare with Santa Clara's, so I would hear the errors if I messed up. Trust me, it was more complicated then, without the aid of computers. This allowed me to unite my love of music and electronics. So yes, it was a success. It actually worked. Unfortunately, I no longer have that recording.

I did it! I graduated from the Connecticut School of Electronics in October of 1976. Then, I began looking for my first technician job. I cannot express the help and support I continued to receive from my immediate family and close friends. It took a while, but I accepted a position at Dictaphone Corporation in Bridgeport, Connecticut. The job was fascinating, but I knew it wouldn't be my forever home. I began checking and repairing recording devices. Later, I assisted engineers with other equipment. Electrical engineering caught my attention early on.

Ed, a very good friend and horn player, called me to talk about the Garfield Cadets Drum and Bugle Corps. He mentioned they may have room for more drummers even though it was late in the season. They had a goal to qualify for the established DCI National finals. They were one of the original founding members of DCI and one of the oldest junior corps, if not the oldest, in the history of the organization. They had made it into the DCI finals for the first time in 1975 but missed in '76 (you needed to place in the top twelve). In any case, my busy schedule made it difficult to add anything. I graduated from Electronics School in the fall. I was now not in top drumming shape, which made performing in any DCI corps highly unlikely. It certainly appeared over. So, I thanked him for thinking of me, but focused on my job and stayed involved in martial arts. But it wouldn't be the last time he asked.

Garfield Cadets

Yet another call from Ed. Finally, after several failed attempts at convincing me… Well… "You're a real good drummer, and you love this stuff. If you don't try now, you'll always wonder about it. It's in your blood! You're aging out after this year. This is it! Your last chance for good. It's getting late in the season…"

I was silent for a moment. "You're fouling me up. I have no freakin' clue if this is even possible! Where would I even live on such short notice? I'd have to drive from Wallingford to New Jersey several times a week and learn everything in a month." "You could live with me and Mom in Trumbull. There's an extra bedroom. You could work in Bridgeport until we tour, then we could commute to New Jersey, until we move. Dee Dee and some others from Connecticut are also trying out."

Man! Was this a moment! I went nuts thinking about it. And because it was Ed, I was really hashing it over. I'm out of drumming shape, and the Garfield Cadets are a top DCI Corps. If they were being paid, they would be considered professionals. My mind was exploding, and there were rumors of layoffs at Dictaphone.

Michael H Fiondella Jr

Naturally, I discussed this with my parents and close friends. "Maybe you should get this out of your system once and for all! Not that you need to stop playing, but maybe you should go," Dad stated. Mom was worried but knew my passion for music, so she was cautiously excited for me. Okay, that's all I needed to hear. I rushed to get back in shape and moved in with Ed. It wouldn't be easy, but I was always up for a challenge.

So, it was game time for me. I packed up. My family and friends wished me luck, and off I went to Trumbull. Mind you, there was no guarantee I would even make the cut. Dee Dee and I met again in April of 1977. It was unusual to join a corps (of this caliber) this late in the season. It was, to say the least, very nerve-racking. I was in a blur and numb. Garfield was and is one of the top DCI Corps, both in the past and now. Garfield's drum line was very young, as far as drum corps experience goes, and they had challenges with Gerry Shellmer's parts. Maybe that's one of the things that gave Dee Dee and me and some a second chance. I placed all my music experience, particularly drum corps experience, on this. Garfield had great members and instructional staff throughout its many years, and 1977 was no exception, as it obtained an outstandingly unique director and instructional staff at that time. Doc Cinzio became Director of the Cadets. He served in that capacity from 1977 through 1978. During his stand, the Cadets had their first extensive tour, covering eleven states in thirty days. Other staff included Frank Dorritie for horns and Gerry Shellmer for drums. Their incredible repertoire was Rite Of Spring by Igor Stravinsky (Chicago Symphony Orchestra), Primal Scream by Jay Chattaway (Maynard

Pieces of Dreams

Ferguson), Star Trek by Alexander Courage, Pieces Of Dreams by Michel Legrand, Echano by Chuck Mangione, and I Don't Know How to Love Him (from Jesus Christ Superstar) by Andrew Lloyd Webber.

Please forgive me for not recalling all the instructors, staff, former cadets, and members who were so heavily involved. Many helped so much throughout the season, including during the unique circumstances in the drum section. I was among a few who, unfortunately, were there for such a short time, wondering if this would even work.

Frank Dorritie may have gotten one portion of music from the studio during or after Maynard Ferguson had recorded Primal Scream. In any case, Garfield had a great drum line at that time, but not at the experience level of some of the other corps for that period. Gerry's drum parts were unbelievable and undeniably incredible, and words could not explain how good these written parts were. The drum section had its work cut out for it, performing these uniquely challenging parts at times. The main drum solo was Dave Brubeck's Blue Rondo à la Turk in 9/8 and 4/4-time signatures. This might have been Gerry's last year writing for drum corps drum lines. Believe me, I really don't care if the drum section had enormous challenges. I would not have wanted anyone else to write the drum parts for that beautiful jazz-like show they had that year. Believe me, I really think most who knew him would agree. No excuses, though; the drum line sometimes had execution issues, which was a large part of scoring in those days. If all the snares don't sound exactly like one—tick! Same with the toms, etc. The only exception would be if separated parts were played intentionally, which would be evident to a drum judge. In any case, I started practicing like crazy.

Many corps would perform songs written by Chuck Mangione. Since Garfield's one song was Echano by Chuck Mangione, another unique memory comes to mind. When he performed at the Oakdale Musical Theatre in Wallingford, I had the opportunity to meet and talk at some length with his father. What a lovely gentleman. He told me some stories and gave me lots of encouragement. When Chuck Mangione was there, at the Oakdale, the theatre had a wooden dome and was a theatre in the round. It also had a round stage in the front and center of the theatre. Many times, when allowed, the stage would be set up to rotate for the audience, allowing everyone to see the show much better. As Chuck performed on the round stage with one of his songs, whoever controlled the circular motion must have set it to turn too fast. Well, then again, it's a lot too fast. Chuck waved for the band to stop in the middle of the song. He approached the microphone and said calmly but confidently, "Would someone please kindly slow this birthday cake down?" The audience all laughed. It was an interesting moment. Later, he became very impressed with the drum and bugle corps performances and was happy to see that many corps performed his music.

Ed and his mom were so gracious. His mom was another angel. I felt so welcomed. With great excitement and nerves, we were on our way to my first meeting at Garfield, New Jersey. I had no idea what to expect so late in the season. This was completely unusual and unexpected. We finally arrived. I exited the car and was introduced to a few members, who welcomed me graciously. Then, some drummers rushed me over, grabbed a snare drum, placed it on me, handed me a pair of sticks, and stuck me in the snare line. I said, "Guys, shouldn't I talk to the staff or drum instructor first?" One of the drummers, probably Jimmy, said, "Quiet, stay still; Gerry is checking the drums." I only thought to myself, Oh boy. The drum line was lined up for rehearsal. I thought to myself, What the heck just happened. I stood still as Gerry Shellmer, a well-known and strict instructor and musical genius, walked down the line to check the drum tuning. Out of the corner of my eye, I saw him eventually approach the snare line to each of the snare drums at the farther end. He leaned over, hummed into the drum head, and turned the tuning key on the drum lugs. He continued down the line, repeating this. He finally got to me, then leaned over to my drum head, humming and tuning the drum.

I stood perfectly still, thinking, what in the world would happen? Then, before he spoke the first words he would ever say to me, he looked straight at me with a cool look on his face, stood for a moment staring, and then, in a serious tone, said to me, "Do you crumple or fold your toilet paper?" The whole line laughed, including me. I would guess he wanted me to relax, which worked for a second. He stepped back and then yelled to the drum line, "Take it from uumph flump flump fla wanna wanna hope a dee daaaa!" Then he counted, "1, 2, 3, 4." The drum sounded like no other, erupting with a power like no other. What a powerful-sounding, rhythmical part, as most of Gerry's parts were. Not knowing anything yet, I was out of place, of course.

What a start! What an incredible sound! The Cadets' drum section really had some challenges that year. I hope I recall this correctly: There was minimal experience for that caliber of drum section that year, and one of the snares may have been primarily self-taught. An unreal situation. Unbelievable for a drum section like this. Also, Gerry's parts were known to be very challenging but absolutely incredible and unique. He wrote some of the best parts, especially for the Cadets' show that year, an astonishing jazz show I absolutely loved. I wish I could explain it. Even though we probably got more ticks than usual, it may have been worth it. I could not imagine any parts better than his for that show. Unfortunately, we did have to water some parts. The drum section and the whole corps wanted to make it to the finals that year. What parts, what synchronization, what accuracy, what sound, and the size and power! Yes, of course, no excuses. The drum section had its challenges, and we certainly didn't want to be the reason for not making the finals. All corps and their specific sections had difficulties over the years, but one must push forward. Every section was impressive!

My impression of all this is based on what I recall as best as I can. They wanted to increase its size as quickly as possible due to the circumstances, which now included some late additions to the drum line. Because of our experience and reputation in Connecticut, we had the rare chance in history to become a part of the Garfield Cadets. It was like all the stars lined up perfectly at one moment. Not by any means was anything guaranteed. There was genuinely much work to be done. This was among the best corps at a Drum and Bugle Corps level. If successful, I was concerned that the few of us would likely become the shortest active Garfield Cadets members in history. I'm not so sure that was a title we wanted.

I was soon taken into a small room with a few veteran Cadets. It was like a condensed summary of a rookie's initiation or audition. This was not the norm. I overheard a veteran Cadet exclaim, "This is nuts." I didn't blame him a bit. Another said, "Do you realize what you are committing to!?" I said, "Yes." He said, "Look, this is highly unusual, but some want to try to increase the drum section quickly, so here's the deal: This corps comes first, and you will learn all the parts and drill within two to three weeks cleanly, or you are out of here!" They also stated some basic rules and regulations. As some older folks might say, this is gonna be a doozy!

Working full-time didn't last long after joining Garfield. However, I saved up enough to pay dues and cover basic expenses. I knew (at some point) I would want to change my job, possibly go back to school for engineering, or maybe even pursue music. This corps experience was my very last chance.

Ed's mom was very insistent about not taking any money from me. I tried so hard to give her something. She was unreal. Ed and his mom treated me like family. It was overwhelming. I had known Ed for some time, and he was always an excellent friend and a great soprano horn player. Now we'd get to know each other much better, as would his dogs! One early morning, I was woken by dogs jumping on the bed. I guess we were friends now, too.

Michael H Fiondella Jr

I gave my two weeks' notice at Dictaphone and knew I would likely return to school again. For now, I was excited and determined to make this work. This was it for junior corps.

At first, we commuted to Garfield, New Jersey. Fortunately, Garfield was in northern New Jersey, making it more feasible to drive from Connecticut. I recall listening to the radio and hearing Dreams by Fleetwood Mac many times during all our rides. Every time I hear that song, it still reminds me of Garfield and the commute. Given the circumstances, it was an ironic title: riding down Route 15 and crossing the Tampen Zee Bridge.

Everyone was welcoming and dedicated like I've never seen. You'd think the whole world was highly into this stuff. Many would discuss how generations of families were members and involved with the Garfield Cadets. It was a completely different world. The drummers gave me the music. I read musical notation, okay, but these parts were challenging. A few drummers, including Jim, wrote out the exact sticking along with the music to help me learn the parts more precisely and speed up my memorization. This would be a massive challenge for the few of us from Connecticut attempting this last-minute feat. As I said, the stars all lined up precisely for us. I can't imagine that ever happening again. Putting the emotion and level of a challenge into words is a challenge. I'm not a professional writer, but I'm using the words I know as best as possible.

As I've also said, Gerry Shellmer's parts arguably were among the best ever written. Even though Garfield's drum line would have some struggles, I am truthful when saying

Pieces of Dreams

I was so glad I could try at least performing with his compositions. I cannot imagine anyone who could have written better parts for Garfield's jazz show that year. I went nuts practicing! They didn't treat me like a rookie, possibly because of the strange circumstances and the fact that I would be aging out that year.

Around May, arrangements were made for us to live with cadet families in NJ to make it easier for everyone. I moved in with the family of a snare drummer, Joe. They were another excellent, welcoming family.

I would practice at every possible moment and be determined to learn these parts as quickly and accurately as possible. It was sometimes unnerving, but I wanted this so badly, so I pushed as hard as possible and kept moving forward.

One early morning, I concentrated on one part to ensure I had it right. No worries, I would use towels or whatever to avoid waking anyone up in the wee hours. I ran to the bathroom that Joe was using and tapped a few parts lightly on the door, whispering, "Hey Joe, is this right?" Then I played a part on the door. He laughed. "Are you kidding me? Wait till I get out of here." "Okay, sorry."

Later, I had to ask the guys, "Where's the part, uumph flump flump fla wanna wanna hope a dee daaaa?" "You'll see. It's in the Primal Scream section from the Maynard Ferguson piece," one answered.

Doc Cinzio, the director, was so welcoming. It was drum and bugle corps heaven. In Garfield, you'd think the entire world revolved around this activity. Another fine drummer, his son Ken, was also in the drum line. We practiced hard to get these parts and attended a few shows before our first performance. Wow! Talk about timing. Just praying and hoping I could pull this off.

Frank Dorrite, another genius, prepared the horn line, and it was like no other. What an unbelievable sound. Just unreal! I cannot say enough about it. Glen, another great horn player from Connecticut, had a solo, along with Drum Major Greg. Chris's solo in the number Pieces of Dreams was phenomenal. I must have listened to it a thousand times. Still, to this day, I play it repeatedly.

Finally, after a few weeks, I had the entire show and drill committed to memory. Boy, did that take some effort? I don't think I was ever this intense about anything. One of the most challenging and rewarding experiences of my life. Now, if I could get through the first show without collapsing.

The first was from left to right: me, Pat, Dave, Jim, Jack, Joe, and Lynn. However, to ensure a smoother transition in our heights, the remaining shows would feature Pat first and then me. Every member was as focused as the next. All were tremendous guys, but Pat and I developed a special friendship. There would be various adjustments throughout the season as needed. Still, all of them worked so hard and were so dedicated.

Before the show, shortly after we were dressed and ready, one of the drummers suddenly grabbed hold of my uniform sleeve and dragged me to where the corps was circled around with some instructors, alumni, and all the members. Then, the corps sang the corps song, "Oh Holy

Name." Talk about getting the chills. We also sang the Amen at the end of our show. It was controversial, but it was an extension of that song. We did this after the judging gun went off to keep with the rules. More on that song coming up.

How did we get that? Amen. Charles Mura, Michael Koeph, and the Rev. Edwin Garrity of the Holy Name Catholic parish in Garfield, New Jersey, founded the Holy Name Cadets Drum and Bugle Corps in 1934. The song, Oh Holy Name, was written in 1937 or 38, and the Cadets quickly became one of the top groups in the country. This song was usually, if not always, sung before and/or after every show. The lyrics are taught to all members and are still used to this day, with alumni joining in to fill the entire area. The feeling exuded is indescribable.

The Song: Oh, Holy Name

Oh, holy name, my holy name, Thy name shall be,
eternally, Thy name shall spread, throughout the land,
and keep it safe, for evermore, when on the trail or on the
march, you'll know that here is holy name, march straight
and true, to victory, for holy name, shall always be,
(repeats), Amen.

    (sung to the tune, O Tannenbaum)

I survived the first show, and now it was time to tweak. I would highly consider this generation of Drum Corps as the pioneers of the modern age. However, we still had a very traditional approach. For me, this was the best way to perform.

So, there we were at another practice... Playing our first number, Tiny somehow missed a beat. Then we saw Gerry start his Olympic sprint, running across the field. Someone said, "Here he comes!" Gerry grabbed the bass from the opposite side of Tiny and yelled, "Dag nab it! The sock! Don't miss that sock!" meaning the accented spot. Holy Moly. Of course, we all took turns making boo-boos. If snare drummer Dave messed up, he'd say, "Ham and Eggs, Baby, Ham and Eggs." If it were Pat, he'd utter, "Uh huh!" Lynn and Joe were always quiet, and maybe they'd let out a sigh. Jim, Jack, and I might say, "What the heck was that!"

Since we were one of the most traditional corps, the guys were required to have short hair but not necessarily shaved heads.

At the end of many shows, as we marched off the field with a cadence or a tap, we'd remove our shakes and hold them in our left hands, with our arms around them. After we removed our shakes, the crowd released a mellow "oooooowwwwww." Remember, there was plenty of long hair in the 1970s.

We were the first to play the Star Wars theme in our warmups (to the best of my knowledge). Garfield would warm up with Star Wars, and then the horns would do some 'all over the place' exercises. The Drum Major would salute (to signal the start), and then the horns, without stopping, would turn and accent right into Rite of Spring by Igor Stravinsky. The judges, usually caught unprepared, would scatter to find errors or tick whatever they could find. That didn't last long as other corps began to protest. Oh well. It was not the first time we would cause controversy that year.

As the year passed, I realized my life as a cadet was quickly ending. The proverbial question was, can the oldest drum and bugle corps in DCI make the Nationals?

Michael H Fiondella Jr

The Tour

Our tour would cover at least nine states during August 1977. We received the surprising news that our primary drum instructor, Gerry Shellmer, could not make the tour. We would have our hands full for sure. This was another miserable and daunting challenge for the drum section.

On August 4, 1977, we left Garfield, New Jersey, at 7 am. We had a detailed list of what to prepare and how, along with a contact list for each stop for everyone who wasn't touring. We only had one location where we slept in dorm rooms, at the University of Denver in Colorado, for the DCI Nationals. At all other stops, we'd be in sleeping bags in school rooms or gyms. Much of our sleeping would be done during our long bus rides. With very little extra time, we would be up very early, eat breakfast, practice, eat lunch, practice, eat supper, practice, and then sleep. This would repeat all month long. Exhausting as it was, we loved it.

And so, in this case, we began our typical summer days. Rise and shine early, short rest, eat breakfast, short rest, practice/rehearse, practice/rehearse, practice/ rehearse, practice/rehearse, short rest, eat lunch, short rest, practice/rehearse, practice/ rehearse, practice/rehearse, practice/rehearse, short rest, eat supper, short rest, practice/ rehearse, practice/rehearse, practice/rehearse, practice/rehearse, relax, and sleep. Repeat and repeat! With little extra time, this would repeat throughout the month. As said, exhausting as it was, we loved it. This was very physically and mentally challenging.

All the top drum corps were indeed highly competitive but still had a deep-down respect for each other. At least, that was the impression I had. Here's one event between the Chicago Cavaliers Drum Corps (which began in 1948) and ourselves (which started in 1934).

Around 1958, the Garfield founding parish stopped supporting its traveling drum corps. However, the members and staff still wanted to be able to travel and participate in competitions. Thus, that year, traveling to Chicago for the Legion Nationals was at their own expense. The members had to use makeshift uniforms and borrowed instruments from the Chicago Cavaliers (a huge thank you to them; nothing personal, but I'd still want the Cadets to score higher). That year at the American Legion Nationals in Chicago, Illinois, the scoring results (out of twenty-eight) were: first place, Blessed Sacrament Golden Knights from Newark, New Jersey; second place, the Garfield Cadets from Garfield, New Jersey; and third place, the Chicago Cavaliers from Chicago, Illinois.

On our 1977 tour, many thousands of spectators attended the DCI Midwest (one of our first significant competitions). This would be one of the drum section's better shows, with the corps scoring sixth out of ten finalists (out of twenty-eight preliminary entries). Our controversial Amen, sung after the judging gun went off, provided another great crowd response. The tradition, dedication, and raw power were infectious. This show will always be treasured because it was one of the loudest crowd responses I ever heard during a performance. The raw power of the drum and horn line and the moving color guard. The thunderous roar at the end of the songs. Goosebumps. I can't explain this feeling.

I would hear Gerry Shellmer's incredible rhythms and unique syncopations. As Gerry might say, "Flaagaaa, flaatyop, sock!" Everything was aimed at perfection: flags hitting the ground and grunts from the corps. Robust, smooth, and so cool, these shows were like nothing else I have ever experienced.

It was so beautiful to travel across the country. But of course, there were times on the long bus rides when we'd get a little punchy.

On a long ride through miles of corn stalks, Pat would suddenly imitate a corn stalk, making corn stalk sounds. How would that look and sound? I wouldn't know how to answer that, but it was extraordinary—you had to be there.

One early morning, Pat had me wake the members to look out the window as he hopped out of the woods like a rabbit. There was nothing like a rookie waking up a bunch of veteran players.

At one restaurant, the drummers sat right near each other. Of course, as drummers do, we played our drum solo with the knives and forks, after which the people applauded.

We will never, ever forget good ol' Aunt Nellie. Nellie DiDomenico. What an absolutely fantastic lady. She started helping Garfield in 1957, and there was one year when the corps was named the Holy Name Cadets. She loved sewing and caring for the uniforms, as well as all the kids. Any cadet, including me, could come to her to fit and fix our uniforms to perfection. She'd help if someone was sick or needed any assistance. I still remember her fitting me when I first received my uniform. Oh, such pride I felt.

We would pass through many places, including New Jersey, Ohio, Wisconsin, Illinois, Tennessee, Arkansas, Texas, Oklahoma, Kansas, Colorado, Nebraska, Minnesota, and my home state, Connecticut. There are so many beautiful places. How fortunate we are to live in the U.S.

As we continued the tour, I recalled a few events in the great state of Texas, and boy, was it hot. Did I say it was hot? Besides the expected practice, I remember two particular events. One was that after one practice late afternoon, we were all shot, hot, and soaked with sweat as usual. It seemed more exaggerated this time. There was a public pool not too far from us. After a practice late afternoon, we asked the young girl lifeguard, "Would it be okay if we just jump in the pool just to cool off, then leave?" She was very friendly and said, "Sure." I remember how nice that water felt.

It was also in Texas, where the DCI show had a clinic for several bands. As we ended a drum sectional practice session, two girls from a local band walked by the drum line. I was in one of those moods and said that if we broke soon, I would introduce them to the drum line for a close-up look if they wanted to. Jim and the crew placed their drums on the ground and said, "Okay, hotshot, let's see what you're gonna do?" Now, please believe me, I'm no Burt Reynolds, and I genuinely hope that if you ask anyone who knows me, they would say I was respectful and treated everyone with dignity. This was just for fun. So, anyway, I ran around the school building corner as fast as possible (my drum corps pals could no longer see me). Then I pasted the two girls, dropped to my knees, and graciously explained my situation, begging them to make me look good. Impressed, they looked at each other, quietly talking among themselves. "Come on, we'll take good care of you." Then, placing their arms around me, we walked back around the corner. Our drum line couldn't believe what had transpired. We all laughed, and the two girls watched, asking questions about our corps.

I'm unsure if I ever admitted that detail to the drum line, but it's out now. All in fun. The girls in the line probably just shook their heads. On that note, I can't imagine what Dee Dee, Lynn, and the other girls thought. They were all very, very talented and very, very special.

Did you ever have an off day? Fortunately, there was only one time I could think of when nothing synced for me. It was actually earlier, before the tour. Gerry ran over to me and shook my drum, saying, "Get with it, man. It's almost show time." He was a great instructor, strict, and, like Mr Sturtze, he expected perfection. I admit I was off and pissed at myself, but eventually was able to pull it together.

Michael H Fiondella Jr

Sometimes, if you don't have any bad luck, you don't have any luck at all.

If you have the time, please check out the eleven-minute show from 1977. I am so proud of our stellar performance. Our repertoire was the resounding loud and clear Rite of Spring by Igor Stravinsky, and it was not a bad drill for those days. Then we moved into Primal Scream by Jay Chattaway (Maynard Ferguson), featuring a funk-like rhythm that sounds like a drum set throughout much of it. From there, it transitioned into a jazz version of "Star Trek" by Alexander Courage. I loved the syncopated phrasing written by Gerry throughout this piece (it was challenging to keep it clean and sounding like one snare). Then, into Dave Brubeck's Blue Rondo à la Turk in 9/8 and 4/4 time signatures. Then one of my absolute, absolute, absolute favorites and favorite memories is Pieces Of Dreams by Michel Legrand. Thank you all, and thank you, Chris, for that superb, incredible soprano horn solo. The brass, in my estimation, is unique and elegant.

Note: Johnny Mathis sang an incredible rendition on the Johnny Carson show, which might be available on YouTube. Maybe Garfield 1977 is, too.

What a beautiful song! I have always loved the way Garfield performed it. The drums may not have been as busy for that number, but what an excellent piece of music. Then we played Echano by Chuck Mangione, and drum major Greg played a soprano solo. Finally, to the number, I Don't Know How to Love Him (from Jesus Christ Superstar) by Andrew Lloyd Webber.

Note: Due to rules, the soprano buglers carried extra horns on their waists so that, in the end, the color guard could retrieve the horns and add to the sound with eighty horns blasting. The guard was taught to play this part.

Then, there was the ever-so-controversial singing of the Amen at the end. This caught the judges off guard. Speaking was not allowed. We did this portion after the gun went off, so it was after the judging portion. The Amen came from our traditional corps song, "Oh Holy Name." The Cadets still learn that song to this day.

As Garfield ventured through the season, we made the necessary adjustments to the show. Tour shows included the DCI Midwest, followed by seven additional DCI competitions. I recall yet another of our all-day practices.

We practiced sectionals as the drum line rehearsed next to the Mississippi River. We returned to the field to practice the entire ensemble and drill as usual after completing the sectional. Anyway, on the way back to the field, the drum lead, Jim, and the Cadet veterans decided to explore a small set of stairs heading into the police station. I'm thinking to myself, this is odd. We all followed as usual. When we arrived, a policeman was behind the front desk window. Then, the drum line marched in place, playing some exercises. It was loud, and I thought, we're in for trouble. However, the policeman looked at us like we were all nuts and slammed the small window. However, we finished the exercise and headed to the field. I know it was strange.

Another rehearsal was a more solemn experience. We were practicing when we noticed a young boy in a wheelchair. He was such a delight to watch as he bounced in his chair with great excitement, clapping at the end of every piece. It was a two-way street—we derived joy from him, and in turn, we made him a delighted boy.

We later heard that the raw power and great sound inspired several kids. Due to our influence, they joined a drum corps the following year.

During one parade, we heard some commotion as we prepared to march. A few of us went to see what was going on. There was clapping and someone yelling, "Hey! "Hey! Hey! Hey!" with several of the cadets from the horn line. Encircled in the middle was a cute old lady dancing and having a blast. When it stopped, everyone hugged her. What a joy to see.

Another time, I noticed a pair of marching shoes on the street. Seconds later, one of the tympani players was seen running back to get his shoes. After the parade, I asked him, "What the heck happened?" "I had to borrow a pair of shoes while my others got cleaned, and these were so big, I walked right out of 'em."

When we required a street rhythm for a few parades or other reasons, we often played Jethro Tull's Thick As A Brick. That was fun and different.

One morning, we surprised Frank Dorrite, our super horn instructor. I don't know how they did it, but they managed to obtain a large number of helium-filled balloons. We banged on his trailer door, and when he answered, we all sang the famous ending of our 1977 show "Amen" and got a great reaction from Frank. Later, he made me feel quite good when he appeared disappointed to hear I was aging out.

I recall the drum line having a short break, and I noticed Gerry Shellmer staring at my pink panther shirt. This shirt had a few holes from wear and tear, but it was one of my favorites, so of course, I still wore it. After a short time, he slowly approached me, admiring my holey shirt. As he stood near me momentarily, many in the drum line gathered around us. He slowly placed his finger in one of the holes in the shirt and hummed the Pink Panther theme in a unique jazz tone, something like: "flagumt flagaaa, flawhop…" Then he slowly walked away. We all cracked up.

I fell asleep at the back of the bus, was out cold, and dreamt that I was in a massive tube spinning at an incredible rate. Then, it was spinning at a ridiculous speed. When I awoke, the bus took a sharp right turn off an exit. I jumped, smacking my head hard on the storage rack above, and yelled, "Ahwwww," falling back into the chair while everyone I woke up threw whatever they could at me. Oh man, what a bummer.

Michael H Fiondella Jr

The DCI Finals

We finally arrived in Denver, Colorado. Such a beautiful place.

Now, we could sleep in the University of Denver's dorm rooms. It was drum and bugle corps heaven. I remember that beautiful lit-up cross on the mountains at night.

While here, you'd think the whole world was involved; at least, that's what it felt like to me. Many people at the forefront of the entertainment industry and sports world began to notice the changes.

Sometimes, I wished I had come to this corps so much earlier. People like snare drummer Lynn and soprano bugle player Gail had joined earlier, and I could see why. Dee Dee had to carry those multiple tenors as well. At times, as we exited our buses or rehearsed, crowds of people would watch.

During the season, several cadets asked me if I was also interested in trying out for the Individual Snare Drum Competition. However, I was not preparing for individuals, as it took considerable effort to learn and maintain Gerry's parts, especially when arriving late in the season.

Nonetheless, I had so much support from special director Doc Cinzio (whose doctor background sure came in handy during the tour) and his sons Greg and Ken (another fine drummer), so I decided to try it.

I needed to put in a request with our drum instructor, Gerry Shellmer, before the tour. "Gerry, may I get your permission to try the DCI Snare competition?" "I don't see why not, but I must check out your solo." I then played an older piece, as time would not allow for a new creation. I liked it. "What do you think?" "I like it, it was cool, ya, go ahead man, that should be okay. Do you want to see my solo?" I was going to hand him my drum and sticks, but he stopped me. "No, man, I don't need the drum nor the sticks. "Huh?" Then, in his cool, Gerry-like manner, he began, "Fla gaaaaaa, flow op, wanna, wanna haba maba cawanna, sock!" (It's a sock for a rim shot, I think.) Then he stopped and said, "I saw this leaf," and I said, "How did that leaf get there? I won by two points. It's cool…" The guys and I stood in amazement with our mouths wide open. He certainly had a way of expressing parts. He was a musical genius who could crack you up simultaneously. Too bad he missed the tour. What a crazy set of circumstances.

A few Cadets approached me and asked, "We heard you do a pretty good Jerry Lewis imitation, including that Nutty Professor, so how about letting loose a little for the corps?" Are you kidding? I need to loosen up." But they goaded me into it. I grabbed my teeth and special wig and let loose before the entire corps. Kind of a go-get-em speech. Even though I was nervous, everyone laughed, and hopefully, I helped them relax.

Pieces of Dreams

The staff spoke to us as we prepared to perform in the preliminaries held in Boulder. Everyone was tremendously excited, and we kept Aunt Nellie busy as usual. I thought, "Wow! I'm about to perform in the biggest show of my life with the greatest and most historic, traditional drum and bugle corps."

Like everyone, I felt prepared, but... We sang our traditional song, Oh Holy Name. We approached and lined up in our competition positions on the field. Then, the formal preparations included the drum major saluting. The pause seemed to continue forever, and the applause was loud, even for the preliminaries. One of the judges must have liked us because he approached the drum sections as we stood at military attention. "Come on, guys, let's keep it tight!"

The anticipation and waiting were over. In my head, it took fourteen years of preparing for these eleven minutes. How profound. Then the gun went off, and we were on our way! We were moving. I know you'll feel the intensity if you ever hear the preliminary recording! Moving! Powerful!

Then, the judges ran everywhere, looking for the tiniest of errors. Everything was scrutinized. Nothing escaped their eyes and ears. The sound from the drum section is wild. Hearing those parts with lots of syncopation! Arguably, some of the most challenging parts were played. It was cool to listen to the sound from this perspective. You hear the tremendous horn section from a distance from this position and see parts of the guard in your peripheral vision moving like crazy, but it's hard to explain. Snares are in rhythm with the toms, tuned bass, cymbals, keyboards, tympani, and other percussion, with everyone working intensely. You hear accents and numerous rhythmic patterns. At the same time, melodies are in the background, sometimes louder and sometimes softer, depending, of course, on the position of everyone and the part of the show. It's a blur, clear, and busy all at once. Catching your breath. Cymbal crash accents, bass drum accents, snare accents, and toms accents are just a lot, with many clean notes, volume, and power. Horns beautifully smooth, horns blasting at times, rifles spinning like propellers and being tossed high in the air in perfect synchronization, hearing that click sounds when the rifles fell into their hands, guard flags being motioned fast all over the place, together, solos and physically moving like crazy. Then, at some portions of the show, particularly at the end of some numbers, the crowd's deafening roar!! Loud roar!! Some would even stand up, and some would scream.

Then, suddenly, it's all over. Those sweet eleven minutes go by in a flash: Pieces of Dreams, the Amen, everything! For us, the preliminaries were complete. It was now out of our control. Now comes the wait. That wait seemed like an eternity. I really believe our preliminary performance was just incredible! I wish I had a video of it.

So we waited and waited. It seems like forever. We needed to score in the top twelve to place in the finals. Forty-five corps are in contention for the top open-class finals. No pressure, right? I was praying and hoping to get this chance to march in the finals. I thought about all the cadets who didn't have this opportunity.

Pieces of Dreams

Our score was announced. 84.45. That put us in 12th place, but the preliminaries were not over. You had to make the top twelve to be in the finals competition. At this point in the preliminary competition, the Kilties would likely be the last corps that might obtain a better score than us. We talked and wondered and waited. Would we still make it? Then... "The Kilties score is 84... point... 4... 5. Huh!!! This would be the first time a tie occurred in the DCI. We were all so overjoyed. I, of course, called my parents and told them to keep an eye out for the televised DCI Nationals. Our corps realized it would have been a no-go had it been one-hundredth of a point less.

Snare individuals approached. Doc Cinzio and a few others took me to the DCI individual area. Another drum corps dream of mine came true. I met Alan and a few others from the Santa Clara Vanguards. At that time, they were one of the best drum lines in the world. A young lady in the group stated, "We are so happy to see Garfield back in the finals again. Can I take a few pictures of you?" "Of course," I said with pride.

We talked and traded experiences, and I asked them about their thoughts on our charts and drum parts. They mentioned how different they seemed. In some fashion, it is different. But they loved them. They loved the syncopation and our jazz-like approach. I was honored to hear this. I explained that years earlier, I had set up my sound system to perform with the recording of their 1975 show, including Entrance of the Emperor and His Court (the parts I played, as I listened to the album, were a little overly complicated for sectional parts, but I should have realized that). They chuckled and said, "We'd never attempt that with a large snare line." Then they added that they would try to catch my individual performance. That meant so much to me.

Then, my turn finally came up. I entered the room and saw some Vanguards, Cadets, other corps members, and judges. I don't recall the exact audience size, but there were quite a few people. I ended up in 6th. Oh well, remember that I was at a considerable disadvantage; the sun was in my eyes (ya, I know, I've used that one before!)

Now, it was off to the final rehearsals and preparations to perform in the 6th annual DCI finals. "Do your best and have fun," our instructors called. It would be televised with host Gene Rayburn (TV personality), co-hosts Helen Rayburn (Gene's wife), and Peter Emmons (known for drill writing).

We entered the field facing a crowd of approximately 30,000 people and a vast camera crew from PBS. It was surreal. I recall hearing Pat say, "Wow." The glitter of the lights reflecting off the horns, all the instruments, and the guards' rifles and flags were beautiful. The sound, the music, the roar of the crowd!

Being the first corps on for the finals competition was undoubtedly a challenge, to say the least. It was often referred to as the sacrifice corps. The show went well, and we ended up in 13th place.

When it came to finally walking on that finals field, it was, and I say again, dreamlike. Talk about timing and fate and luck and determination and so many things. A moment that I will never forget. How could I ever give enough thanks to my family, friends, God, and all the Garfield Cadets of all time? I was in the right moment, at the right time. It's hard to believe it all came to fruition. That final show was a blur.

It was indeed Pieces of Dreams for that mere eleven minutes—years and years of experience for a brief moment. It was over. It went by so quickly. How fortunate I was. I was a seven-year-old kid hoping to perform.

After the show, as some of us walked behind the bleachers, some young kids asked for our autographs. They might have been joking, but they were serious. Again, an honor. What are those worth now? No answers are necessary! I'd rather stay in the state of wonder, a legend in my own mind.

Michael H Fiondella Jr

Moving On

Traveling and rehearsing tapered off. We still had a few shows, including the American Legion Nationals and the VFW Nationals, but not all the top corps competed. We placed second to the Crossmen at the American Legion Nationals out of eleven finalists out of thirty-three. We placed third out of twelve finalists, with seventeen participants, at the VFW Nationals. We fared well but were nearing the end of the season.

Ironically, my final experience would be in my home state of Connecticut, where I had played earlier with other corps. Out of ten competing corps, we placed third. I certainly was fortunate and grateful, and I was delighted to see everyone. Still, I didn't want this music experience to end. After the show, I met with my parents, who told me how much they loved it. They were pleasantly surprised at the level we had reached.

On a sad note, I would say my goodbyes to many in the Garfield Cadets, hoping to see them again someday. As a competitor, I would sing the corps song for the last time and then leave for home. Garfield's Director and other staff knew this was my final departure.

Exhausted from the month-long tour, I slept like a rock. The following day, I was ready for another tour. But, of course, this was no longer in my itinerary. Strange indeed. I began searching for a new job and also investigated the possibility of returning to school.

Then, I received a phone call for one last hurrah. I packed my Roger's white pearl drum set and other percussion instruments and headed out with the Garfield Cadets to White Plains, New York. We would perform at the New York Civic Center as a warm-up exhibition before Maynard Ferguson and played some of his songs. They even allowed me a small drum solo. Oh, how I long to hear a recording.

After my last (no, really, my LAST) performance with the Garfield Cadets, I was reminiscing backstage with my friend Louie from the Emerald Cadets. Then, a young fellow said hello, complimented me, and gave me some great pointers and advice. "Thanks. Hey, wait a minute, aren't you Peter Erskine?" I jumped up, shook his hand, and returned the compliment. I was so appreciative. He was generous and personable. If you're unfamiliar with drumming greats, Peter Erskine is a phenomenal drummer.

Then, as I was getting ready to pack my car, Maynard Ferguson said a very friendly hello to Louie and me and asked how we were. While we were talking, Maynard's band started playing. "Excuse me for a minute, fellows," then proceeded to the stage, and the audience went nuts. He played some high notes that made the dogs bark. Then, he returned to wish us well as the audience cheered on. The only thing I could think of was holy moly. Louie, what do you think?" "I might just start using my horns as

Pieces of Dreams

bookends," he laughed. My last adventure. What a magnificent end to a several-year adventure. I was excited but melancholy.

The Garfield Cadets was an extraordinary period of my life. Unfortunately, I still need to place my name on the alumni list as I write this. It may seem odd, but since I was only involved briefly, I never justified putting myself on that list. However, it's on my to-do list. Another unusual thing is that I rarely attended drum corps shows after I left. It may be hard to believe, but it was too difficult to watch without performing. That's just me, I guess. The few shows I could see were memorable, especially when I would hear and join in with "Oh Holy Name"—what a wonderful tradition it has been since the late 1930s. I will never forget the ending to our 1977 show, Amen.

You can usually tell the difference immediately if you hear a drum corps, band, or music in the distance. Years later, my wife would experience this with me when we visited my in-laws.

As we drove down their driveway for another fantastic dinner, my wife, kids, and I were greeted by the sound of musical chords from the high school just down the street. I usually don't react like this, but I told my wonderful wife, "Please take the kids inside. I'll be right back. That's a bugle corps practicing at Amity High School." She looked at me, surprised. I drove to the high school, not realizing there was a drum corps show in the area. As I pulled into the parking lot, what do you think happened? The corps hit their last note, which ended their practice session. Would you believe it was the Garfield Cadets practicing at Amity

High School? I couldn't believe my luck. I spoke with many members and staff. What a pleasant surprise.

To many, drum and bugle corps may seem very insignificant. To many, it's just a kids' pastime. An event that occupies several days per week during the off-season involves summer tours, traveling, and practicing hard for eight to twelve hours daily. And an event that requires physical dexterity and dedication—an event that is misunderstood. Anyone involved would likely be shaking their heads in agreement. Hopefully, those who weren't better understand what it might have been like. When it's in your blood, it's in your blood, and hearing those unique sounds anywhere at any time evokes something in you that's difficult to explain.

I'm sure many drum corps enthusiasts think I should have included other examples. Still, I am confident that everyone will understand that including everything is nearly impossible. I taught briefly, and I am very proud of my students. Hopefully, I left a small piece of something with each of them. I'm not done with music; I'm simply taking a hiatus.

Just a very few more last-minute other thoughts… Steve Gadd (a famous drummer), who was in a drum and bugle corps, used a portion of the drum solo, a kind of Crazy Army, for a well-known song. I want to express my appreciation to Les DeMerle (a remarkable drummer), who encouraged me during the creation of my 1989 two-hour instructional video, The Fundamentals of Drumming (Emphasizing Rudiments). Countless thanks to my wife, Jennifer, for her endless support throughout the twenty-four-hour recording (it was more affordable to do it this way).

More lasting memories: The Santa Clara Vanguards in 2009 performing Ballet for Martha (Simple Gifts). The Phantom Regiment 2003 Harmonic Journey and the expression on the young lady's face at the end of the performance. Of course, I must mention the Garfield Cadets' 1987 Appalachian Spring, the first corps to repeat with three DCI titles. Garfield Cadets' Holy Name will always hold a special place in my heart.

Thank you for letting me share memories near and dear to my heart. Years ago, in my competitive years, I thought it would be all for nothing if the Garfield Cadets didn't make it into the DCI finals competition. Now, I realize this is far from true. Trying has worth, no matter the outcome. I might have been one of the shortest active competitive members of the Garfield Cadets—not the most excellent title to acquire. Nonetheless, I was in the right place at the right time and had the right experience with all the right people. Our drum line had its talents and challenges that year, and those of us from Connecticut tried to help. Hopefully, we did. So many paved that road before me.

My family gave me opportunities that I could have never dreamed of—opportunities they could have never had—freedoms and choices that I could have never dreamed of. My family went through so much to give me every chance possible. I was just a seven-year-old, dreaming of performing in a big show. It took fourteen years to perform for eleven minutes in the DCI Nationals Competition.

Ironically, I probably read fewer books than anyone I know, and here I am attempting to write a book—likely my only one. I believe and hope that my music will ultimately become my strength. I hope to offer my kids and other readers a different perspective.

So there you have it, a tiny part of my young life—a beautiful and one of my all-time favorite songs in the Garfield Cadets' 1977 repertoire, Pieces Of Dreams. I thank God and all. For Holy Name Shall Always Be, Amen.

Epilogue

On March 29, 2024, I emailed the Cadet organization a long-overdue letter requesting to be added to the alumni page. Receiving no answer, I sadly realized that the unthinkable had occurred—on April 2, 2024, the Cadets had folded, filing for bankruptcy.

I may have missed names, but I want to thank all the cadets of all time. Also, many thanks to all the good people everywhere for helping me keep hope, faith, family, and young memories. Special thanks to Pat and George for their kind words, which I came across on the internet. This adventure was indeed Pieces of Dreams. Keep the hope! Keep the faith.

Michael

"There is always an excuse to do the wrong thing and a reason to do the right thing." MHF

"If there is no God then nothing matters but if there is a God then everything matters, keep faith." MHF

$\infty - c = \infty$

Pieces Of Dreams (POD) Notes

Los Angeles Times
Nov. 13, 2008
By Valerie J. Nelson
Article: Jay Fiondella dies at 82; flamboyant owner of Chez Jay made the restaurant a Santa Monica landmark

The Hollywood Reporter
November 10, 2008
By Mike Barnes, The Associated Press
Article: Jay Fiondella dies at 82

Santa Monica Daily Press
By News
August 18, 2011
Article: Flamboyant owner made Chez Jay a landmark

Pieces of Dreams (the song)
Composer: Michel Legrand
Lyrics: Alan and Marilyn Bergman

www.drumcorps.marines.mil
United States Marine Drum & Bugle Corps founded November 9, 1934

Wikipedia
Drum and bugle corps (classic)
Drum & Bugle Corps History
Mark T Sheehan High School - Information on history

Nard.us.com
National Association of Rudimental Drummers
History/Information

https://www.fromthepressbox.com/
Drum Corps Scores

https://www.dcxmuseum.org
Marching percussion in the 20th Century
By Lauren Vogel Weiss

Oh Holy Name: Reference: Garfield Cadets

Alumni Drum & Bugle Corps - https://members.tripod.com/donna_darrigo/id22.htm)

Cadets 2023
Part of the Cadets show last year with the drums emphasized. One of the closest videos I could find to experience what it's like being in the drum section. What a great job they did!

Cadets 2023 - Learn the Music - Intro

Cadets 2023 - Learn the Music - Closer

Editor's note: Since it's not practical to type full hyperlinks in printed books, I recommend searching for any of the following words on YouTube.

"Cadets drumline" "DCI drumline" "DCI finals" "Garfield Cadets" "Emerald Cadets", etc.

www.ingramcontent.com/pod-product-compliance
Lightning Source LLC
Chambersburg PA
CBHW060749050426
42449CB00008B/1330